POWER GRAB

Obama's Dangerous Plan for a One-Party Nation

POWER GRAB

Obama's Dangerous Plan for a One-Party Nation

by

DICK MORRIS & EILEEN MCGANN

Humanix Books

www.humanixbooks.com

Boca Raton, FL, USA

Power Grab: Obama's Plan for a One-Party Nation
© 2014 Humanix Books

Humanix Books
P.O. Box 20989
West Palm Beach, FL 33416
USA
www.humanixbooks.com
email: info@humanixbooks.com

Humanix Books is a division of Humanix Publishing LLC. Its trademark, consisting of the words "Humanix Books" is registered in the US Patent and Trademark Office and in other countries.

Printed in the United States of America and the United Kingdom.

ISBN (Hardcover) 978-1-63006-026-8
ISBN (E-book) 978-1-63006-027-5

Library of Congress Control Number 2014942786

Contents

Introduction

"All legislative powers herein granted shall be vested in a Congress of the United States, which shall consist of a Senate and House of Representatives."

— US Constitution, Article I, Section 1

PRESIDENT BARACK OBAMA, the former constitutional law professor, is at war with the United States Constitution.

It's just not working for him.

He simply can't get Congress to pass his expensive, expansive, big government, nanny-state agenda. Congress is not buying it. Not at all.

So what's a president to do? Obama is a left-wing president who is desperately determined to impose his radical agenda to transform our democratic government and free market economy into his socialist-style ideal before leaving office in 2016. He's a president who is obsessively fixated on keeping the left in permanent power by turning our two-party system into a one-party monopoly.

For Obama, drastic times called for drastic measures. So, the solution for President Barack Obama was an easy one. He decided to embark on an outrageous and sweeping scheme to decisively — and illegally — grab power away from the Congress and appropriate it to himself. Under the guise of "executive action," he would legislate without the interference of the legislative branch. Under the guise of enforcing the laws, the president would, instead, selectively *refuse* to enforce the laws. And ultimately, under the guise of reasonableness, the president of the United States would, instead, become utterly intolerant and unquestionably dictatorial. He'd rule on his own.

That's where things stand right now. Barack Obama has snatched the legitimate constitutional powers of Congress and invested them in himself. He's illegally exercising them every single day, in every conceivable way.

And he has no plans to stop anytime soon. Make no mistake about it: We need to stop him. Immediately. Because he's getting bolder and bolder. So, our first step must be to win the Senate in 2014. But that's only the beginning. That will keep him at bay for two more years. But our most urgent task is to keep the Democrats out of the White House in 2016. Our energies, money, and passion must be relentlessly focused on electing a Republican president. Because if we fail in 2016, Obama's successor will be emboldened to continue the Obama power grab — and we cannot afford the consequences.

If there's any doubt about just how pervasive his usurpation of congressional power has become, take a look at his repeated brazen actions throughout the disastrous implementation of ObamaCare. Without either the permission or agreement of Congress, and without any legal authority to do so, Obama singlehandedly revised important sections of the Affordable Care Act (ObamaCare), substantively amending, changing, reversing, modifying, and even ignoring parts of a valid act of Congress — *on his own.*

There's no question that it would always be much easier for a president — any president — to just decree his favorite policies as law, like a king, or a dictator. That would eliminate the tiresome democratic processes that require consulting with Congress, compromising, and providing time and opportunity for citizen input. Reaching out and grabbing the power of Congress is so much more efficient — no hassles, no personalities, no drama . . . and no compromises.

But it's also illegal and unconstitutional. And the president of the United States knows that. He knows that he's in charge of making sure that the rule of law is followed, not ignored. Article II, Section 3, of the Constitution unconditionally requires the president to "take care that the laws are faithfully executed." But Obama is doing that selectively. If he approves of a law, there's no problem. But if he doesn't, he matter-of-factly changes it or ignores it. In those cases, there's no such thing as "faithful execution." To the contrary, there's a faithless disregard for the law and an inexcusable dishonor of the Constitution.

That's understandable when you realize Obama's disdain for the parts of the Constitution that don't work for him. At a private fund-raiser in May 2013, Obama made an amazing statement and took "a swipe at the Founding Fathers," blaming his inability to move his agenda on the "disadvantage" of having each state represented equally in the Senate.[1]

Apparently, he would prefer the big democratic states to have more votes than the smaller Republican ones. The law professor president seems to have forgotten our history and the protracted debate that resulted in the mandate of two senators from each state.

But at least he's consistent. It's always someone else's fault. Now it's not just the Republicans and the Tea Party and FOX News. *It's the Founding Fathers, too!*

How We Can — And Must — Stop Him

This book will explain in detail how Obama's dangerous power grabs threaten our liberty, our economy, our livelihood, our values, and our very future — and why we must stop the ongoing end run around the Constitution by the Democratic Party. Because the only way that we can restore our democratic system and guarantee our freedom is to get the Democrats out of the White House in 2016. Nothing short of that will work.

And the campaign to elect a Republican president must begin this very minute. It can't wait another day. It's that urgent; it's that critical. Now is the time to act.

I've been in the White House. I've run successful presidential campaigns. I know what's involved. It takes planning, focus, organizing, and patience. And, most important, it takes a strategy tailored to the unique circumstances of the country and our politics at that moment.

IT'S TIME TO DEVELOP A POLITICAL GUERRILLA WAR

Here is our strategy: To wage a new kind of political guerrilla war, battling Obama — and defeating him — each step of the way, each and every day. Throughout this book, we will describe each of Obama's outrageous power grabs, assess its impact, and explain the game plan for the guerrilla war we must fight to stop his tyrannizing of America. We have no choice. As we look around at our political circumstances, it's clear that this election cannot be just like any other election. The stakes are way too high.

The new political guerrilla war must be waged house-to-house, hand-to-hand, as we battle each and every regulation, executive order, statutory interpretation, and procedural change to protect our cherished democracy and its vital system of checks and balances. And we will have plenty of ammunition. Obama never stops usurping his power, acting illegally, and endangering our freedom. We'll have lots to work with. And, by the time we reach 2016, the reputation of the Obama administration must be in tatters and the democratic candidate must feel the unsupportable weight of the heavy burden of succeeding and defending it. And we need to keep following the likely democratic candidate,

Hillary Clinton, never letting up in our bombardment. We have to hold her responsible for America's global weakness. We've got to show how she allowed, authorized, and permitted wiretapping by the NSA of foreign leaders to go on. Americans have short memories. We've got to underscore that ObamaCare was originally HillaryCare and explain how this fundamentally flawed system is her handiwork — her dream. We've got to remind the voters about her history.

And then comes the final battle. We must explain to America how each of these power grabs robs every one of us of our chance at the American dream and takes away our aspirations for the future. We have our work cut out for us.

Join us. Our lives depend upon it. Winning the Senate is no substitute for a victory in 2016.

The congressional victories of 2010 made it evident that our ultimate goal has to be nothing less than taking back the presidency. Remember, after 2010, Obama was emboldened to embark on his lawless power grab.

If he couldn't control Congress, he'd ignore it. So control of even both houses of Congress won't suffice. It's just not enough to stop Obama's rogue governing.

But it is the first step toward our final goal. With a victory in the Senate, even with Obama still in the White House, there is a lot that we could accomplish. We could:

- Stop him from confirming the appointments of rubber-stamp judges who will repeatedly ratify his power grab.

- Make it impossible for him to do an end run around Congress by using international treaties to control guns, eliminate fossil fuels, erode our sovereignty, and control the Internet.

- Rein in his spending. Since the president cannot veto line items in the budget, control of both houses gives us power of the purse.

- Form coalitions with Democrats to pass legislation Obama opposes, bridling in the NSA, ending his war on coal, controlling our borders, and blocking the release of dangerous criminals.

But beyond these specific areas, a smashing defeat of Obama's congressional minions will constitute a repudiation of his administration, highlighting his shortcomings and accentuating his failures. That's what we need to do.

ObamaCare: One Giant Power Grab After Another

ObamaCare is the best example of Obama's illicit power grab. Since the more than two-thousand-page bill passed Congress in 2010, (apparently without anybody reading it), the Obama administration has taken twenty-two separate actions to amend it on its own, according to the Galen Institute.[2] These presidential encroachments on congressional privilege fundamentally altered important sections of the ObamaCare legislation in order to mask the incompetence of his own administration, kowtow to the dictates of his liberal constituents, and cave in to the extraordinary demand to restore federal health care subsidies to members of Congress and certain congressional staff that had been expressly and knowing repealed.

Think about that last point for just a minute: Members of Congress, making a minimum of $174,000, are once again eligible to receive financial subsidies to pay for their health insurance premiums under an exemption quietly granted by the Office of Personnel Management with the president's support. It doesn't matter that the ObamaCare bill allowed nothing of the sort. In fact, Senator Charles Grassley's (R-IA) amendment specifically required members of Congress and their staff to purchase health insurance on the exchanges, which effectively eliminated their generous federal subsidies. Grassley wanted the people who were imposing ObamaCare on the rest of us to be personally familiar with just how it worked — or didn't — and subject to the same potential premium increases. That certainly makes sense. Maybe Congress would be a lot more concerned about solving the problems associated with ObamaCare if the members were covered by it. But they didn't want that and made sure that the requirement, which had the effect of an appropriations bill, was repealed without ever reaching the floor of Congress. That's a blatant power grab.

So why did this happen? Because our representatives wanted special treatment and Obama personally involved himself in the efforts to placate them. So now there's special treatment for those special people who didn't even bother to read the ObamaCare bill before they voted for it. But once they ultimately did read it, they quickly sprang into action to benefit themselves. They didn't seem to be too worried about the rest of us. And Obama didn't hesitate to go along with their self-serving demands. As a result, under ObamaCare, there is literally one standard for members of Congress and another one for the rest of us because Obama decided to take matters into his own hands and make his own laws. That's just one of the many illegal actions that he's taken on ObamaCare. Chapter One provides a full discussion of them, but below is a summary of his other actions:

- Issued fourteen executive decrees to delay the statutory mandates of the Act enacted by Congress

- Changed the terms of the statute regarding cancellation of policies

- Changed the Medicare Advantage program

- Enacted a rule to permit tax credit subsidies for people who got coverage through federal exchanges, even though the Act only permitted it through exchanges established by the states

- Closed enrollment in the high-risk pool

It's important to remember that the president is not legally able to make these critical changes. Only Congress has the legal authority to legislate and Congress certainly never agreed to the extensive modifications made single-handedly by the White House. But that never concerned the law professor president. He's defying the Congress, flouting the Constitution, and doing just about whatever he wants, without any legal basis.

Susan Campbell, Chairman of the American Civil Rights Union noted in her statement opposing the president's actions on ObamaCare: "Nowhere in the Constitution does it say that Congress gives up its designated legislative authority whenever a president decides to legislate on his own."[3] But Obama isn't concerned about what either Congress or the voters think. He's forging ahead with making his laws and ignoring existing laws, no matter who disagrees.

As President Obama well knows, his willful power grabs — on health care as well as on dozens of other issues — are unconstitutional, unlawful, and ultimately, unsustainable. For it was to Congress alone, in Article I, Section 1, of the Constitution that the original framers clearly granted the sole power to make our laws.

Note to Obama: The United States Constitution does not bestow a parallel legislative power to the president. Nowhere, no way, no how.

But that quintessential premise of American constitutional law, so familiar to even a first year law student, hasn't moderated the constitutional lawyer president. To the contrary, he's adamantly asserted a singular power to make laws on his own, and, in some cases, to even determine the constitutionality of existing federal law without the benefit of a court ruling.

Now that's a power grab.

Not surprisingly, Barack Obama makes no apologies for his flagrant violations of the constitution and his interminable insistence that he absolutely has the authority to do so. In fact, when pressed about it, he's downright arrogant. Confronted by *The New York Times* about objections to the delay of the employer mandate by members of Congress, he replied; "I'm not concerned about their opinions."[4]

And that, unfortunately, is the truth. The president couldn't care less about what Congress thinks. He thinks he knows better. Actually, he knows he knows better. That's what's really frightening about what he's doing. The constitutional lawyer in the White House has no respect for either the constitution or the rightful powers of the other branches of government. And he surrounds himself with equally insufferable advisers who pontificate on his expansive executive authority and threaten to use it on everything from climate change to school nutrition.

Enter The Power-Grab Czar, John Podesta

To help implement his lawless strategy, Obama appointed a temporary *power-grab czar*, John Podesta. His actual title, counselor to the president, belies the true nature of his portfolio. Podesta is the adult in the Obama White House charged with devising a multitude of strategies to bypass Congress and maximize Obama's executive power during the year 2014.

Podesta was a brilliant choice to execute Obama's misguided power grabs He is one of the most well-connected Washington insiders who intimately knows the powerful players. He's had experience all over town: as a lobbyist, top congressional staffer, White House aide, and ultimately as Bill Clinton's White House Chief of Staff. In 2003, he founded the influential liberal think tank, Center for American Progress (CFAP), populated with many former Clinton White House and campaign staff. His talents are in great demand. For example, although he supported Hillary Clinton in the 2008 election, Obama appointed him to head his Transition Committee and advise him on appointments and policies. And, while Hillary Clinton was secretary of state, he served as a senior advisor and continues to do so now. In addition, his brother and sister-in-law, Tony and Heather Podesta, are two of the most successful lobbyists in Washington, with client billings of $27 million and $7 million,[5] respectively, from the top corporations in the United States. No doubt about it, Podesta knows his way around.

But even more important than Podesta's experience and contacts is that he is a true believer in the legitimacy — and urgency — of Obama's executive power grab. And he is not the least bit afraid to taunt Congress about the president's plans to step on its actions. In May 2014, for example, he rather untactfully told reporters that Congress "could not derail the Obama administration's efforts to unilaterally enact policies to fight global warming."[6]

Them's fighting words!

Imagine: An unaccountable temporary employee at the White House brashly telling Congress that it cannot derail the president's unlawful activities!

Podesta smugly elaborated on the likelihood of Congress' success in taking any actions to thwart the president's lofty wishes: "All I would say is that those have zero percent chance of working . . . We're committed to moving forward with those rules."[7] ("Those" rules, by the way, would be Obama's rules.)

Zero chance to stop the president from taking illegal actions? That's the message to Congress from the White House. Does it sound like an invitation to work together, or does it sound like anything other than a blatant power grab?

That is exactly what it is. It wasn't meant to be conciliatory. It certainly wasn't a call for unity. To the contrary, it was meant to be an in-your-face assault — a proclamation by the president of the United States, through his unelected and unconfirmed czar, to illegally steal the power of Congress.

Obama and Podesta are engaged in a high speed race to grab whatever they can before the November election. Their deadline is a firm one for several reasons. First, they want to use their executive actions to try and fire up the liberal base to increase turnout in November of 2014 in a last ditch hope of avoiding a monumental debacle at the polls. Second, they want to grab as much as they can before the very likely Republican trouncing on Election Day 2014. All of the major polls have consistently predicted that the Democrats will not hold on to the Senate after the next election. If the polls are accurate and the Republicans win the Senate, any subsequent attempts at power grabbing by Obama would be much harder to engineer and maintain. So time is of the essence. And, finally, Obama desperately needs to show that he can accomplish something — anything — in his second term. So far, he's basically accomplished nothing.

He's now trying a very different tack, hence the hiring of John Podesta. No more Mr. Nice Guy! With or without Podesta, Obama's actions are nothing less than an audacious, breathtaking, and yes, unprecedented power grab — a chilling and conniving plot to thwart the Constitution and exercise unlimited and unchallenged authority.

Podesta has been a strong proponent of the "ignore Congress" theory that Obama has eagerly adopted. In 2010, he authored a study that advised the president to do just that and take bold executive action on everything from jobs, housing, trade, health care, education, taxes, to foreign affairs without bothering with the Congress.[8]

In the final months of the Clinton White House, Podesta put together a series of a few executive and regulatory actions that bypassed Congress on such issues as prohibiting development on certain parts of federal lands, including the construction of roads, logging, or exploring for coal, gas, or oil.[9] The few late-term Clinton executive actions were by no means a bombardment that triggered concern. Before that, most of the Clinton Executive Actions were generally uncontroversial and dealt with issues traditionally at the core of a president's executive power, like implementing acts of Congress that require coordinated action by federal agencies, such as Clinton's 1995 order for all agencies to cooperate in collecting delinquent child support. As a result, for example, the Treasury Department refused to issue tax refunds to deadbeat dads and sent the money to the states to distribute to their families. There were a few unusual uses of the executive power, but Clinton was definitely not in a stampede to take away congressional power at every turn. Some compare Clinton's and Obama's executive orders. But that's like comparing apples and oranges. Clinton's elaborated and codified acts of Congress. Obama's replaced them and acted in their stead.

But now, the president and his czar have big plans for government by fiat. Nothing is beyond their reach.

It appears that the community organizer and constitutional law professor has morphed into the imperial president.

Apparently, President Obama now believes that the legislative power, delegated only to the Congress, can simply be seized by him and switched over to the executive branch at his will. Think about it: The president of the United States has openly announced his intention to subvert the Constitution by circumventing Congress and making laws and policies himself. And he's proud of it.

Obama's illegitimate premise is antithetical to our democratic form of government. It's alien to our well-established principle of limiting the power of each of the three branches of government so that no single one becomes overly powerful and infringes on the others. That's the very definition of balance of power. But, Obama has turned that concept upside down and inside out. He's contemptuous of anything and anyone who tries to curtail his personal and political power. It's blinding him.

In his zeal to institutionalize his leftist vision of America, Obama is determined to bypass Congress, seize its powers and govern without them. He won't ask for the advice and consent of the Senate if he doesn't feel like it. He won't ask for legislation if he has to compromise. He will unabashedly, unapologetically act on his own. Listen carefully to Podesta's words. Translation: Get Lost, Congress. I'm in charge.

Using a variety of existing tools — executive orders, presidential memoranda, and federal regulations — Obama has arrogantly created a parallel legislative branch that ignores Congress and usurps its powers. These are powers that the Constitution does not allow Congress to delegate.

The indispensable American principle of separation of powers that is so fundamental to our democratic system of checks and balances has become simply an inconvenient obstruction — an annoying bump in the road in Obama's steadfast resolve to impose his radical policies, no matter what.

So, it's his way or the highway. And right now, our historic doctrines of checks and balances and separation of powers are way out there in the slow lane of that Obama-is-in-charge highway.

James Madison, author of the Bill of Rights and drafter of the Constitution, warned about the dangers of concentrating power in any of the three branches of government:

> The accumulation of all powers . . . legislative, executive, and judiciary in the same hands, whether of one, a few, or many, may justly be pronounced the very definition of tyranny.[10]

James Madison, Federalist #47

And it is now time for us to heed Madison's prescient message.

On a daily basis, Obama is ignoring the Constitution, mocking the very idea of separation of powers, and scorning our system of checks and balances. And without any respect for those important pillars of democracy, our freedoms and our rule of law are at risk.

Obama's brazen maneuvers are nothing less than a cynical executive power grab designed to aggregate power in his Oval

Office. This is exactly the kind of concentration of power in one branch of government that Madison warned us about; it is the kind that leads to tyranny. It is the kind we need to stop.

This book will outline the unlawful actions underlying Obama's shameless power grab and the consequences of his illicit actions. We'll explain his cynical political motivations and his opportunistic goals. Finally, we'll make recommendations about what has to be done to stop him — now!

But, first, let's examine how this all started.

Obama: I'll Act on My Own

It was shortly before the beginning of his second term in January 2013 that Obama laid down the gauntlet, using his weekly radio address to announce: "When Congress isn't acting, I'll act on my own"[11] Obviously, Obama and Podesta, along with the boys at the White House, had been crafting Obama's tough new message for his next term. Several days later, at the first Cabinet meeting of his new term, the president elaborated on his plans:

> We're not just going to be waiting legislation . . . I've got a pen and I've got a phone . . . And I can use them to sign executive orders and take executive actions and administrative actions.[12]

He meant business. Forget the Constitution — it's Obama at the helm, alone, isolated, and grabbing more and more power away from Congress and giving it to the White House each and every day. He was assuming power that rightfully rests in the legislative branch of government, not in the Oval Office.

It wasn't always this way. Before he was elected president, Obama didn't support the broad use of executive power. In fact, during his first campaign for president, while campaigning in Lancaster, Pennsylvania, then Senator Barack Obama sharply criticized President Bush and took exception to his executive actions:

I taught constitutional law for ten years. The biggest problems that we're facing right now have to do with George Bush trying to bring more and more power into the executive branch and not go through Congress at all, and that's what I intend to reverse when I am president of the United States of America.[13]

But that was then and now is now. Safely reelected, President Obama has made a dramatic turnaround. Now, he boldly asserts his absolute right to take matters into his own hands and, in effect, rule by fiat, arrogantly threatening to use his "pen" and his "phone" to bypass Congress if they dare to disagree with him.

He knows better and he's admitted that publicly. In fact, only recently, he lectured supporters who urged him to bypass Congress on immigration that such a course was illegal. While on a speaking tour in November 2013, he was accompanied by David Remnick of *The New Yorker*, who reported on two exchanges with immigration reform activists who demanded that Obama take executive action to stop deportations. On each occasion, Obama carefully cautioned about the constitutional constraints on the use of executive power. At one event, a heckler yelled out, "Executive order!" suggesting that Obama circumvent Congress. The crowd warmly applauded in agreement. But, in his response, Obama cautioned them about the grave constitutional limitations he faces.

> Before everybody starts clapping, that's not how it works. We've got this Constitution, we've got this whole thing about separation of powers. So there is no shortcut to politics, there's no shortcut to democracy.[14]

Amen, Mr. President.

At another event on the same day, a young man interrupted the president, shouting "I need your help . . . our families are separated . . . You have the power to stop deportations for all."[15]

The president responded with a message the young protestors undoubtedly did not want to hear, patiently explaining why he could not — and would not — simply use his pen to eradicate our national immigration problems.

Obama told the audience, in no uncertain terms, that he did not have the power to stop deportations by executive order, saying:

> . . . if I could solve all these problems without passing laws in Congress, then I would do so . . . But we're also a nation of laws. That's part of our tradition . . .[16]

Yes, Mr. President, it is not our tradition for the president to violate the law, but that's precisely what you are doing. But it's not just our tradition that demands it; it's much more than that. Our Constitution demands it. Section 8 of Article I of the US Constitution undeniably confers on Congress, not the president, the power "to establish a uniform rule of naturalization."[17] But despite the president's unquestionable acknowledgment of the illegality of solo presidential action to change deportation law, and despite his righteous claim that as president he would not break the law, he has done just that. Since Obama took office in 2009, there has been a 43 percent decrease in the number of deportations though the courts.[18] And shortly before the 2012 election, the president announced an executive order that basically implemented the provisions of the DREAM (Development, Relief, and Education for Alien Minors) Act that Congress had refused to pass. He's not waiting for Congress to give him any authority.

The executive order immediately stopped deportations of young illegal immigrants who came to the United States with their parents before they were sixteen and have lived in the United States for at least five years, are in high school or are high school graduates, and have no criminal records. According to the Pew Hispanic Center, some 1.4 million people might be covered by the order.[19] Since then he's expanded green card eligibility to include the spouses of high tech workers in a program that is overrun by corruption. And he's expected to offer DREAMers the opportunity to enter the military and gain a path to citizenship.

Although Obama doesn't practice what he preaches, there's no question he knows that what his massive power grab is doing is in direct violation of the Constitution. He just doesn't care.

Why Is Obama Trying To Seize The Power Of Congress?

There are a number of reasons why Obama has decided to take the process of making laws into his own hands.

The first reason is simple — because he can! He's president of the United States and he thinks that can do anything. And, for the most part, he can.

When guiding French President Hollande on a tour of Thomas Jefferson's Monticello home in February 2014, Obama made a telling remark: "That's the good thing about being president, I can do whatever I want."[20]

And, he does! Like many of his predecessors, Obama has become enthralled with the trappings of power that surround his office. Think about it. Start with his personal life. The president of the United States lives in the most luxurious home, under the most luxurious circumstances in the world. According to the White House Curator, there are 132 rooms and 35 bathrooms. The White House Executive Residence is exquisitely decorated and filled with priceless antiques, paintings, and decorative art. In fact, the president and first lady can borrow any paintings or sculpture they wish from the National Gallery and hang them in the Residence. Past presidents have adorned the walls with original paintings by Monet, Degas, Jackson Pollack, and other old and modern masters. Bouquets of beautiful fresh flowers and orchid plants tastefully adorn the tables of every room.

The staff for the residence includes almost one hundred people devoted entirely to the maintenance and upkeep of the building and the First Family. Truly, every wish is their command. There's a theater for first run movies, a pool, tennis courts, gym, and even a bowling alley for leisure time. There's also a beauty salon, florist, and in-house physician. Traveling is no problem. Planes, helicopters, and limousines are at their disposal. While billionaires and oligarchs may have their own state of the art planes and limos, they can't stop traffic. They can't close down airports until their planes take off. But the president can and does do that every day.

And while the First Family lives in the most elegant and beautiful house in the land, the Obamas don't have to pay for much with the president's salary of $450,000 a year. Other than their personal food and dry-cleaning, just about everything else is on the taxpayers.[21] Even laundry and mending, stationery, books, subscriptions, newspapers, and leftovers from State Dinners are free. The taxpayers also cover the costs of maintenance, entertaining, travel, and personnel. How much does all of that cost? Well, the annual budget request for the residence in 2013 was $13,200,000. That's a pretty exceptional lifestyle, especially for a couple that arrived only a few years after the two paid off their student loans.

The downside of all of that glamour and luxury is that the president exists in a small isolated bubble and loses touch with any normal lifestyle. Combine the personal perks that are only rivaled by Buckingham Palace with the deference shown to the president by anyone and everyone who comes into contact with him — in the White House, at planned events, in meetings with foreign leaders, and you have a recipe for a self-absorbed belief in your own infallibility.

That's Obama's place right now; he is certain that only he is right and certain that he should act on it. That's just what he's doing . . . because he can.

Advancing His Socialist Ideals and Pandering to His Liberal Constituents

Obviously another major reason for the constant power grabs is to advance the policy ideals that are reflected in the executive actions. That's important to Obama. He needs to keep his coalition of single women, African-Americans, Latinos, union members, and young people involved and interested. That's why he carves out power grabs that benefit each and every group and keeps them in his camp.

Trying to Permanently Change the Electorate

But the most important reason for his power grabs is to realize his relentless goal of changing the electorate from a two-party political system to a one-party government, dominated by the Democratic Party. That is what animates and excites him. That is what the power grabs are all about.

This frightening goal will be discussed in great detail in Chapter One. This is what we must fight.

How Does He Do It?

How, exactly, is Obama improperly seizing congressional power? By an overreaching, illegal, and unconstitutional abuse of executive power that deliberately undermines the historical congressional authority to make laws and to advise and consent to the president's appointments.

Obama firmly opposes the preservation of the separation of powers that has served as the cornerstone of our democracy for more than two hundred years. His actions make that clear. Why is this separation of powers so important? Because, as George Washington University Law Professor Jonathan Turley skillfully reminds us, it is critical to our liberty:

James Madison fashioned a government of three bodies locked in a synchronous orbit by their countervailing powers. The system of separation of powers was not created to protect the authority of each branch for its own sake.

Rather, it is the primary protection of individual rights because it prevents the concentration of power in any one branch. In this sense, Obama is not simply posing a danger to the constitutional system; he has become the very danger that separation of powers was designed to avoid.[22]

Without a strict and enforced separation of powers, the threat of tyranny and the loss of freedom increases exponentially.

Congress Won't Stop Him Anymore

What started this imperious tactic? Very simply, it was the refusal of the Republicans in Congress to roll over to Obama's extreme legislative proposals on climate change and immigration, for example. He's taken that rather personally.

Over the past few years, Obama watched, helpless and frustrated, as the guardians of our liberty in Congress shut the door on his chilling blueprint to revolutionize America by transforming it from a free market economy into a stagnant European-like welfare state controlled by the federal government. And his sinister scheme to transform the electorate into a permanent Democratic Party majority by pandering to its every special interest group was never embraced by Congress.

Instead, over and over again, Congress has denied him *carte blanche* and declined to gratuitously pass everything and anything he wants. He now knows this: There will be no blank check sent from the Capitol to 1600 Pennsylvania Avenue. Not now, not any time.

And that has infuriated the president of the United States. He's not going to stand for this. He's been outraged because the checks and balances inherent in our democratic system were actually working to curb his outlandish agenda. By refusing to bow to his every whim, Congress, the legislative branch, effectively limited the power excesses of the executive branch by rejecting the president's radical agenda. But not according to Obama. He sees it much differently.

There are two diametrically opposed views of why Congress will not routinely rubber-stamp Obama's initiatives and appointments. To Congress, its refusal to roll over to the Obama juggernaut is a fundamental element in its responsibility to check and balance the president's power. To Obama, it's simply obstructionism. But, however you define it, Obama has been stopped by Congress in his race to enact sweeping national laws in his dream of an entitlement-driven, government economy.

But, that doesn't mean that he's given up on his fanatical goals. Not at all. When Congress refuses to embrace his objectives, he'll circumvent them. After the Republicans took over the House of Representatives in 2010, Obama began to see the writing on the wall. That's when he decided to fundamentally change the game. If Congress wouldn't play ball with him, he'd find another team — his own team: one that is not in any way dependent on Congress.

From then on, Obama began consolidating the power of both the executive branch and the legislative branch and headquartering it inside one big Oval Office. He's been on an ever-expanding power grab since then. He was more cautious before his reelection, but now, all bets are off.

Obama's Schemes

Obama has a variety of schemes to implement his unlawful power grab. Here's a list of his favorites:

- Create "laws" without Congress

- Waive mandatory deadlines set by Congress

- Selectively enforce laws

- Make "recess appointments" when the Senate is not in recess

- Amend statutes by presidential order

- Refuse to defend existing laws and label a law he disagrees with as unconstitutional without waiting for a court to act

- Appoint "czars" to influence policy and determine regulations — without Senate confirmation

- Issue burdensome regulations

Sometimes he simply ignores — or unilaterally changes — legislation that he doesn't agree with. Selective enforcement of federal laws has become the signature of his administration. If he doesn't like a statute, it's history.

But, legally, the president does not have the option of unilaterally reversing an act of Congress. As former New Jersey Judge Andrew P. Napolitano has noted: "The Framers intended American presidents to enforce all the laws that Congress has written, even those they dislike . . ."[23]

Changing the Statutes Himself

Think about his solo decision to end the deportation of illegal immigrants on his executive order, which essentially implemented the DREAM Act for aliens under age 25, and which Congress had deliberately refrained from passing. Without any action by Congress, Obama revolutionized our national immigration policy. He'll be doing this more and more.

Selective Enforcement of Laws

At other times, he refuses to enforce existing laws that are incompatible with his liberal agenda. Without any direction from Congress, those laws simply cease to exist. That's what happened when Attorney General Eric Holder directed federal prosecutors to permit defendants to argue for lower sentences in drug related cases based on proposed new guidelines that had not been approved by either Congress or the Sentencing Commission — the only ones with the authority to do so. Although Holder is responsible for enforcing our laws, he has decided to personally pick and choose the ones he'll uphold. It's up to him and Obama, not Congress.

Here's a good example: In August 2013, Holder unilaterally announced that the Justice Department would no longer charge defendants with crimes that triggered long sentences under the mandatory guidelines authorized by the US Sentencing Commission and enacted by Congress. Holder, with the support of Obama, decided that the mandatory sentences were just too harsh and decided to act on his own and essentially repeal the tough drug sentences.

It was not until eight months later that the Sentencing Commission formally approved the changes. At the same time, it publicly rebuked Holder for usurping the authority of Congress and the Commission. Judge William B. Pryor, a member of the Sentencing Commission who sits on the 11th Circuit Court of Appeals, lambasted Holder, saying that his "unprecedented instruction [to US Attorneys] disrespected our statutory role, 'as an independent commission in the judicial branch,' to establish sentencing policies and practices . . . and the role of Congress, as the legislative branch, to decide whether to revise, modify, or disapprove our proposed amendment . . . the law provides the executive [branch] no authority to establish national sentencing policies based on speculation about how we and Congress might vote on a proposed amendment."[24]

Congressman Bob Goodlatte (R-VA), chairman of the House Judiciary Committee, commented on Obama's unconstitutional encroachment on congressional power. "Over the last year, we have all witnessed an extraordinary level of executive overreach by the Obama administration. Time after time, this president has pushed the limits on executive power beyond their constitutional boundaries."[25]

And, even supporters of changes in the sentencing guidelines deplored the administration's unwarranted tactics. Michael Mukasey, a former judge and attorney general under President George W. Bush said, "I generally agree with the goal of getting rid of mandatory minimums," said Mukasey. "But the way to do that is to pass a law."[26]

Obama and Holder, Not Any Court, Declare Laws Unconstitutional

In February 2011, shortly after the new Congress was seated with a Republican majority in the House of Representatives, the White House embarked on one of its first bold steps in its calculated road to unilateral presidential action. In an astonishing move, Obama directed the Attorney General to stop defending the Defense of Marriage Act, known as DOMA, which permitted states to refuse to recognize same-sex marriages.[27] Although Obama had advocated the repeal of the law, his Justice Department had appeared in court and defended the existing statute for the two previous years (as it was required to do). But all that changed very suddenly.

The case of *Windsor v. United States*, filed in the US District Court in November 2010, apparently came to Obama's attention and he decided to do something about it. But he didn't make any public announcement that he was no longer going to enforce the law.

In a February 23, 2011, letter to Speaker of the House John Boehner, Attorney General Eric Holder announced that he and the president had concluded that DOMA was unconstitutional and would no longer be defended by the Obama Department of Justice.[28] This was an astounding legal position. Think about it: without any finding by any court that the law was unconstitutional and without Congress repealing the statute, the president had single-handedly decreed the current law-of-the-land to be unconstitutional.

The Supreme Court noted in its opinion how unusual it was for the Attorney General to send a letter indicating that it would not enforce the law when there had been no adverse ruling. The Court pointed out that letters of this sort are generally written when a statute has been struck down by a lower court and the AG can either continue to uphold the law until the Supreme Court acts, or send a letter indicating that it will not defend the law until the Court acts. But here there was no action at all by any court. The decision addressed the unilateral basis for the AG's unorthodox approach:

"The letter instead reflected the Executive's own conclusion, relying on a definition still being debated and considered in the courts that heightened equal protection scrutiny should apply to laws that classify on the basis of sexual orientation."[29] It was a double whammy: The president had, in one unsanctioned stroke, expropriated the carefully defined and segregated legislative and judicial powers for himself.

The president was now acting as Congress, the Supreme Court, and the president all rolled into one.

Not surprisingly, many members of Congress were alarmed by this massive overreach of presidential power. Representative Lamar Smith, (R-TX), Chairman of the House Judiciary Committee, understood it completely. "It is a transparent attempt to shirk the department's duty to defend the laws passed by Congress . . . This is the real politicization of the Justice Department — when the personal views of the president override the government's duty to defend the law of the land."[30]

Ultimately, the US Supreme Court held that DOMA was unconstitutional in its application to federal benefits and required the federal government to apply federal tax laws equally to both same-sex and traditional marriages. But the outcome is irrelevant to the power grab. Obama had no way of knowing how the Court would rule and no prerogative to declare any act of Congress unconstitutional. He could argue it in a court; he could veto a bill that he believed to be unconstitutional, but he had absolutely no legal authority to take over the role of the judiciary. But that didn't stop him.

The president's maverick actions illustrated the base political nature of his power grabs. At its core, Obama's directive to the country's top law enforcement official to blatantly ignore established federal law was an opportunistic political decision.

It was not grounded in a moral belief in the illegality of the law. It was simply a deliberate and cynical pandering to a vital constituency.

According to a new book by Pulitzer Prize winning author Jo Becker, *Forcing Spring*, Obama and his team were calculating the political costs and benefits of supporting gay marriage and feared taking such a position would upset a carefully construct-ed balance in the coalition that he needed for reelection. But by November 2011, the need for some bold action by Obama was evident to his advisers. Timing was the only issue.

When the *Windsor* case caught their eyes, it was already mak-ing its way through the courts. A series of frantic conversations followed with Obama ordering Holder to find a way to justify refusing to defend the DOMA.[31] The Justice Department was distressed enough to call the plaintiff's lawyer and ask them to delay the case because the Attorney General needed more time![32] Ultimately Obama and Holder decided to completely back off defending the federal statute. That's right. The president of the United States ordered the chief law enforcer of the American government to ignore the existing law. They would simply an-nounce that it was unconstitutional.

What Do We Need The Courts For?

Isn't this just the kind of power grab that Madison feared and labeled as tyranny?

It didn't stop there. Within a few months, the White House had institutionalized its scheme for a massive power grab, cen-tered on the theme of "We Can't Wait." The president advised his staff to come up with a program to escalate the use of all possible tools to circumvent Congress and legitimize his pol-icy plans. It was an aggressive, deliberate in-your-face tactic to usurp the powers of Congress. And there was no concern about violating the separation of powers doctrine. William M. Daley, then White House chief of staff reported, "The president expressed frustration, saying we have got to scour everything and push the envelope in finding things we can do on our own."[33]

And push the envelope they did!

Obama: If Congress Won't Control Guns, I'll Put the Gun Sellers Out of Business

President Obama has not tried to hide his fury that Congress would not pass his strict gun control legislation. He's decided to ignore the legislators and go for the jugular.

The Washington Times reported that gun sellers claim that the Obama administration "is trying to put them out of business with regulations and investigations that bypass Congress and choke off their lines of credit, freeze their assets and prohibit on-line sales."[34] Hundreds of gun sellers suddenly found that they were targeted by Justice and Treasury Department rules that literally put many of them out of business. They see it very clearly as an end run around the Second Amendment.

Kelly McMillan, whose family has operated a gun business for four generations, said, "This is an attempt by the federal government to keep people from buying guns and a way for them to combat the Second Amendment rights we have. It's a covert way for them to control our right to manufacture guns and individuals to buy guns."[35]

Federal regulators are now labeling gun sellers businesses as "risky" and that makes it difficult for banks to deal with them.

And now Obama has directed executive branch agencies to purchase massive amounts of ammunition. The Department of Agriculture, the Weather Bureau, the Social Security Administration, the post office and other agencies that would seem to have no need for firearms are now buying tens and even hundreds of millions of rounds of ammunition. Second Amendment advocates charge that Obama is trying to dry up the supply of ammo in gun stores to gain backdoor gun control.

Republicans in Congress are working to undo the Obama administration's war on the Second Amendment.

Recess Appointments

Frustrated by his inability to convince Congress to confirm his three appointments to the National Labor Relations Board, Obama decided that the Senate was in recess and made the appointments while the senators were away for a four-day break. The Constitution allows the president to make temporary appointments while the Senate is on recess without asking for confirmation until it returns. The provision was fashioned at a time when it took months to get the Senate together after a recess. But, in this case, the Senate did not actually take a recess. Instead, it declared itself in *pro forma* ("for the sake of form," or as a formality) session and met every few days precisely to thwart Obama from making any recess appointments.

The Supreme Court held a hearing on the issue after two lower courts ruled against the White House power grab, and a decision is expected before the end of the Court's 2014 session. One of the issues before the Court was who decides, for purposes of a recess appointment, whether the Senate is in recess — the president or the Senate. Even Obama's liberal Supreme Court appointee, Elena Kagan "suggested that it is the Senate's role to determine whether they're in recess."[36] For once, Obama's power grab just might not work. A ruling against the NLRB could result in the invalidation of hundreds of decisions made by the Obama appointees).

Judging by the skeptical comments of the Justices, there is a very good chance that the recess appointments will be thrown out.

Stay tuned.

Promulgating Expensive Regulations

Obama is overwhelming us with needless, expensive, and pervasive regulations. According to the Heritage Foundation, there have been 157 regulations promulgated since he took office in 2009, costing $73 billion every year![37] Heritage says this is twice as many as George W. Bush implemented, and the cost is three times as much.[38]

Businesses are stifled by the excessive regulations and the costs and complexity of the rules are costing jobs. This must stop.

The following chapters will elaborate on each of the Obama power grabs and their implication for all of us.

It's time to fight. Join us in the battle to beat back the serious risks to our country's values and our freedom.

PART I

Obama's Goal:
One-Party Government

Is Barack Obama's flagrant power grab part of a cynical strategy to turn America into a one-party nation? A permanent *Democratic Party* nation?

Is his goal merely a short-term fixation on a democratic win in the next election, or is he playing for keeps, trying to make sure that his party never loses an election in the foreseeable future?

Wherever you look, the evidence unquestionably points to the latter. Without a doubt, Barack Obama is not just looking for good results in (although he definitely wants that, too). Instead, he has a shocking new vision for America that transcends any specific election. What he has been secretly engineering is nothing less than a bold framework for an enduring control of the United States government by the Democratic Party. He wants to put the Republican Party out of business. That's what it's all about.

To achieve that audacious objective, he's concocted an ingenious master plan to marshal all of the powers of the federal government within his reach to create an environment that favors, attracts, and consolidates Democratic Party voters. It's breath-taking in its scope.

And, for the most part, it's based on an illegal and unconstitutional power grab of a magnitude that has never been seen before in more than two hundred years of our democratic government.

He's developed a twenty-first century Machiavellian blueprint for dramatically and decidedly changing our political system.

It's a new paradigm based on simply ignoring the constitution and grabbing whatever policies he can to deliver to his liberal constituents to bind them to the Democratic Party. It's been done covertly, with each of the component parts of the project scattered so far and kept so separate that it is almost impossible to see the parameters of the entire project and understand it as a whole. But the big picture is there and we need to pay attention to it. It's like a mosaic made of many discrete but integral parts that ultimately result in a clear image when joined as a whole. Once the many elements of Obama's cynical plan are exposed, his manipulative intent will be quite obvious.

That's precisely what we are trying to do in this book. We want to expose his power grab for what it's all about: changing the face of America. And we want to urge you to do everything you possibly can to elect a Republican in 2016.

Throughout history, we've often seen authoritarian dictatorships ruling through pseudo-political parties that are really just instruments of their own ego and will. By using tactics that Obama himself has adopted, such as voter fraud, intimidation of the media, regulatory control that emasculates opposition groups or parties, flooding the electorate with guaranteed supporters, and ignoring congressional checks and balances, they rule their nations — no questions are ever asked — and in those foreign countries, the would-be questioners are discredited or land in jail.

But there's another possibility, and that's the one Obama is promoting. Without ever becoming a dictator, a leader of a democratic government could still permit relatively free elections, but, at the same time, effectively manipulate the playing field so that only one party — his party — could ever win.

And that's exactly what Obama is scheming to do.

That's where America is heading. It wouldn't be the first time. We've had periods of one-party governance before. In fact, originally there were no political parties in our new nation. It was only later, when various factions needed to garner support for their national policies, that the American political party system was created. But that two-party system, inaugurated by Alexander Hamilton (Federalists) and Thomas Jefferson (Republicans, also known as "Democratic-Republicans"), quickly faded. The Federalists, who had been the earliest supporters of the Constitution, were discredited by flirting with treason in opposing the War of 1812. Several years later, in 1816, Rufus King was the party's last presidential candidate. After he was trounced by James Madison, the Republican candidate who received 183 electoral votes to King's 34, the Federalist Party folded up. For the next few years, the Democratic-Republicans were overwhelmingly in power, controlling the White House and 85 percent of the Congress.

It was called the "Era of Good Feeling" because of the long stretch of national unity and absence of endless political squabbles. But it but proved to be merely an interregnum in nonpartisanship. By 1832, there were once again two parties. The Whig Party had emerged as an alternative to the Federalists, nominating Henry Clay to oppose the reelection of the authoritarian Andrew Jackson, leader of the Democratic-Republican Party.

There have, been, of course, other periods in which one party seemed to have an irreversible hold on power, but there was nothing in the system to rig it in favor of one party over the other. It was the will of the electorate. Both parties vigorously contested elections and each rightfully believed it had a chance to win. The power was routinely handed over from one party to the other, sometimes for extended periods of time.

After the Civil War, the Democratic Party fell into disrepute for its opposition to the war and was unable to elect a president from 1860-1884. Republicans dominated the postwar years, but the Great Depression extinguished their hold on power. It was the Democrats, under FDR and Truman, that next seemed invincible, and they controlled the White House from 1933 until 1952, when Eisenhower brought their monopoly to an end.

But Obama's determination to create a perpetually dominant Democratic Party is not at all like any of the other periods of one-party rule. What is significantly different about Obama's ambitions for single-party rule is that he is intentionally making it happen. It is not the will of the electorate; it is his conscious rigging of our system, from the composition of the electorate to the voting system, the rules of the Senate, and even the federal budget, to assure that only his party will win for decades to come.

To do this, he is using a ten-part strategy to achieve his goal:

1. Enforcing only those laws he wishes to enforce and disregarding his constitutional obligation to make sure that all laws, not just the ones that are supported by his core constituents, are faithfully enforced

2. Issuing executive orders that far exceed the powers of the president and usurp the functions of Congress and the states

3. Unilaterally changing our immigration laws to allow a virtually guaranteed flow of new, democratic voters into America who will ratify his hold on power

4. Challenging laws enacted by states to prevent voter fraud and institutionalizing ballot stuffing to downscale, left-wing voters to maintain control

5. Using the agencies of the federal government to intimidate, audit, weaken, and cripple the funding sources of the Republican Party, to ensure that only his party survives

6. Expanding entitlement programs to embrace a majority of Americans, he is creating a have-not political party that increasingly pays no taxes, does not even seek work, and gets checks from the government

7. Ignoring the rules of the US Senate on appointments, he has obviated the checks and balances on presidential power that have been built into our system over two centuries

8. Intimidating the media and limiting the freedom of the press that is a vital guarantee of our liberty

9. Rigging the rules of union elections, to expand the reach and power of organized labor to include more American workers

10. Eliminating the Electoral College

A quiet scheme — called the National Popular Vote Movement — has been gradually gaining force outside of public view to change the way we elect presidents in order to maximize the power of big city, democratic machines and the opportunity for voter fraud. This power grab would fundamentally change our Constitution without having to formally amend it.

We elect our presidents now, not based on the popular vote, but by using the Electoral College. Each state is assigned a number of electors equal to the number of its Senators and Congressmen combined. (The District of Columbia, having no congressional representation, gets three electoral votes).

The electors may vote as they choose, although most states require them to vote for the candidate who carried their state.

Only four times in our history has a candidate won the popular vote, but lost the Electoral College (1824, 1876, 1888, and 2000).

But now Democrats are asking state legislatures to pass legislation requiring their state's electors to vote for the winner of the national popular vote, regardless of who carried their own particular state. These laws will take effect and become binding on the electors when states whose electoral strength represents a majority of the Electoral College — 270 votes — have passed similar laws.

Once that happens, the Electoral College will remain in the Constitution, but as an anachronistic appendix — a mere formality. With a majority of the electors committed to voting for the winner of the national popular vote, the Electoral College won't matter.

The formal procedure for amending the US Constitution requires the assent of two-thirds of the House and the Senate and the concurrence of three-quarters of the states (as expressed by the majority vote of their legislatures). But the National Popular Vote Movement seeks to drastically bypass that procedure. Congress would not even be consulted and enough states to constitute a majority of the Electoral College — not three-quarters — would be needed to pass the change.

This backdoor approach to amending the Constitution has never happened before in our history, but Obama's plans to grab power know no limits. That's why we have to end the democratic control of the White House in 2016.

So far, ten states with 161 electoral votes have passed this bill — New York, Hawaii, Illinois, Maryland, Massachusetts, New Jersey, Washington State, Vermont, California, and Rhode Island. The District of Columbia has also agreed. Legislation has also passed one house in a number of other states.

While most of the support has come from Democrats, some Republicans have been fooled into supporting the measure. The Republican-controlled State Senate in New York, for example, passed the measure in 2014.

How would the legislation give the Democratic Party an advantage?

Under the current system, the focus of any presidential campaign usually quickly boils down to a handful of swing states — Florida, Ohio, New Mexico, Colorado, Nevada, Iowa, Indiana, North Carolina, New Hampshire, and Pennsylvania — where history has shown that either party has a chance at victory.

As a result, presidential candidates tend to ignore even populous states whose vote is a preordained conclusion. Democrats know they will carry New York, Illinois, and California and Republicans are equally certain they will prevail in Texas so there's no point in campaigning there extensively.

That's why the really large, powerhouse, democratic, urban political machines — Chicago, New York, San Francisco, Baltimore, Detroit, and the other large California cities — rarely get much funding or attention from national campaigns. Of course, the Republicans, too, carry their share of cities, but most of their strength is concentrated in more rural areas.

Look at a color-coded map of political preferences in America. You see vast swatches of red (Republican) and only a few dabs of blue (Democrat). The democratic vote is highly concentrated in a number of large urban areas.

But if were we to choose our presidents by popular vote, these urban centers would be much more important, and Democrats would work hard to bring out the maximum possible vote. Turnout in inner cities would soar and Republicans would be at a great disadvantage. And the opportunities for fraud would multiply. If the entire election ever comes down to a single state or a mere handful (as happened in 2000), scrutiny will fall heavily on the votes in each corner of the swing state. Voter fraud will be hard to conceal since every ballot box in the state will be under a magnifying glass. But if the national popular vote were to be the deciding factor, voter fraud would be much harder to catch, as it would be throughout the entire nation. Every urban machine in every state would struggle to maximize its vote, sometimes by fair means and sometimes not.

Recognizing this reality, the Republican National Committee voted unanimously to recommend to state legislators that they oppose the National Popular Vote Bill when it comes up in their jurisdiction. But Obama's people will continue to push it. Should the Democratic Party ever win heavily at the state legislative level, look for it to emasculate the Electoral College.

Martial Law

There's one more big issue to worry about.

President Obama has issued an executive order allowing him to govern the country and its entire economy by martial law in the event of a national emergency. While other presidents have had this inherent power, this chief executive's blatant usurpation of powers not granted to his office in the Constitution raises grave concerns over how he would use this unprecedented authority.

We are far away from storm troopers marching through the streets of our capital. The next election is not going to be canceled. Those we elect to Congress in 2014 will be permitted to take their seats. But, beneath these trappings of democracy, Barack Obama's long-term strategy is proceeding to limit its functioning in practice and guarantee his own and his party's perpetual control.

Let's examine each element of the Obama strategy for ongoing political domination and dominion.

Point 1: Enforcing Only Those Laws He Wants To Enforce

Article II, Section 3, of the US Constitution provides that the president shall "take care that the Laws be faithfully executed."[1]

But President Obama has turned that requirement on its head. Instead of fulfilling his constitutional requirement to enforce all laws, he selectively enforces only some laws, depending on how he personally feels about a particular statute. Those he agrees with are enforced, but those that do not square with his own leftist political agenda are completely ignored. Instead of faithful execution, we now have faithless disregard for the law of the land. This passive refusal to enforce *all* of our laws is a key part of his power grab.

Immediately after his election, Obama and the Democratic Party were in control of both houses of Congress and had a sixty-vote "super-majority" in the Senate. He could pass anything he wanted to. But he lost his super-majority in the Senate in January 2010 with the election of Scott Brown to fill Ted Kennedy's seat. After he lost control of the House in the elections of 2010, his taste for the checks and balances of a democracy wore thin.

Instead of obeying the Constitution, he started to flout it. Throughout this book, we will point to examples of his legislating through executive orders and presidential actions without congressional approval. But equally as disturbing is how he achieves his agenda by *not* enforcing laws he doesn't like.

During the Nixon administration, Congress (still in democratic hands) would routinely pass spending bills that the president opposed. Denied the ability to veto individual line items in those spending bills, President Nixon repeatedly resorted to the practice of "impoundment," where he would refuse to spend money that Congress appropriated.

As part of the post-Watergate rollback of presidential power, Congress deliberately terminated the president's ability to impound funds in the Congressional Budget and Impoundment Control Act of 1974.

Now, President Obama is applying a variant of impoundment as part of his power grab. He is not merely withholding Congressionally appropriated funds, he is refusing to enforce laws passed by Congress and signed by the president, even when they don't involve any financial matters.

Obama has made an art form of selectively deciding when to follow the law, oddly seizing power by not exercising the very duties he is charged with. He has constituted himself as a kind of second congress, deciding which laws apply to the term of his rule and which do not. The Constitution confers no such power on the executive, but he has seized it anyway.

For example, after Congress failed to pass the DREAM Act to granting legal status to illegal immigrants who had arrived here as children with their parents, he simply ordered the immigration service to stop deportation of people who would have been covered by the act had it passed.

When Congress voted for sanctions on Iran to prevent it from developing nuclear weapons, the president refused to enforce them for many months. When Iran agreed to limit its nuclear program, the president threatened to lift these same sanctions on his own, by simply not cracking down on countries that violate them.

Despite the clear language of the welfare reform law that only actual employment would satisfy the statute's work requirement, President Obama unilaterally decided that job training or education would suffice to allow benefits to flow.

As states across the nation relaxed their prohibition against marijuana and both Colorado and Washington State legalized the drug, President Obama chose to direct the DEA and the Justice Department to refuse to enforce existing federal law, which prohibited sale or possession of the controlled substance.

The signature accomplishment of President George W. Bush — the No Child Left Behind Act of 2001 (NCLB) — has become an unrecognizable mutation of its former self, as Obama has granted waivers to two-thirds of the states allowing them not to comply.

At issue is its central requirement that all students be proficient in reading and math by 2014 and pass the standardized tests to determine whether the goal has been met. *The New York Times* asked whether the "decade-old program has been essentially nullified."[2]

In place of the Bush standards, the Obama administration has allowed states to promise to set new targets aimed at preparing students for colleges and careers. *The Times* reports that "they must also tether evaluations of teachers and schools in part to student achievement on standardized tests."[3] The No Child Left Behind Act has been criticized for forcing an obsessive focus on test scores, triggering cheating and setting standards that are so high that schools cannot possibly meet them. But without any action by Congress amending the law, Obama has simply granted states waivers permitting them to completely ignore the statute.

So much for taking care that the laws be faithfully executed.

This tendency toward unilateral executive branch decision-making, overriding laws of Congress at the president's whim has been most frequent where Obama's signature Affordable Care Act is concerned. Despite having written the ObamaCare law and managed its passage, the president and the Department of Health and Human Services have been profligate in ignoring its provisions, granting delays, waivers, and out-right reversals of some of its key provisions. (See the ObamaCare chapter for specifics.) Even as his power grab gave him control of heathcare — 17 percent of our economy[4] — he has sought even more power by altering ObamaCare to suit his every whim without even asking Congress.

A key element of our democracy is that the laws passed by one Congress and signed by one president apply for all time until they are formally changed or repealed by Congress and the president. Why is this important? Because every element of our society has the right to be on notice about what the ground rules are for living in our society. We have the right to a clear understanding of our rights and responsibilities as citizens. The rule of law is essential to a stable society and a functioning economy. Without it, the potential for chaos and corruption are enormous.

Obama has suspended this essential pillar of democracy. Instead of a guaranteed rule of law that applies to everyone, Obama has transformed our system of jurisprudence. Now, a law is a law if, and only if, Obama wants it to be a law. It doesn't matter if it has been passed by Congress or has been ruled on by the Supreme Court. If Barack Obama decides he doesn't like a law, then it is no longer a law. Laws may be in effect one week and tossed out the window the next. Selective non-enforcement of federal laws and regulations is a proud centerpiece of Barack Obama's power grab.

It's a dangerous power grab that jeopardizes our heritage of freedom and must be stopped. Only when we have a Republican replacing him in the White House can we feel safe.

Point Two: Obama Uses Executive Orders To Legislate Without Even Asking Congress

Faced with a Republican House and a Senate that was nominally democratic, but ham-strung by GOP filibusters, the president resorted to a much-publicized, executive order strategy in which he proposed to act on his own to change the nation's laws "with or without Congress."[5]

Liberals had long been outraged by the difference between the sentences for crack and cocaine. These disparities, which some said reached to 100:1 ratios, punished crimes involving crack more severely than crimes involving cocaine.

In 2010, the Democratic Congress passed legislation to reduce the disparities, but Obama wants to make the reduction retroactive so as to free up to 12,000 inmates in federal prisons on charges of crack possession or sale.[6] Congress has refused to move on his request to free crack users sentenced under the old law, so President Obama is preparing to use his power of pardon and clemency to release thousands of former crack distributor inmates from federal prisons.

Just as Obama is overriding Congress' authority to pass laws, he is boldly disregarding the power of the judiciary to impose sentences, using his pardon and clemency powers to vitiate sentences imposed by trial court judges and often sustained on appeal.

Deputy Attorney General James M. Cole has asked defense lawyers to help the government locate such prisoners and to encourage them to seek clemency. In December, 2013, President Obama commuted the sentences of eight federal inmates who had been incarcerated under the old rules.

But Mr. Cole wants many more to be freed. He told the New York State Bar Association: "There are more low-level, nonviolent drug offenders who remain in prison, and who would likely have received a substantially lower sentence if convicted of precisely the same offenses today. This is not fair, and it harms our criminal justice system."[7]

The Justice Department asked prison officials to spread the word among inmates that the jail door could swing open for thousands of crack offenders.

Attorney General Eric H. Holder, Jr. said the prison system accounted for 30 percent of the Justice Department's budget, which strained the department's ability to conduct its other law enforcement missions. Of course, neither Obama nor Holder speaks of the huge cost of re-arresting those who have been released, which regrettably, is substantial. According to the Bureau of Justice Statistics, one-third of those released from prison in 2005 were right back in prison again in six months. One-half were incarcerated within a year of their release. Two-thirds were back within three years, and three-quarters were returned to cells within five years.[8]

But because Holder and Obama want them released now, they won't wait for Congress to act and are grabbing the power to set them free right away, circumventing the legislative branch once again and using executive power to rewrite the rules.

It didn't stop there. As the momentum for gay marriage developed across America, President Obama was intent on using his executive power to grant same-sex couples the same status as heterosexual couples enjoy, even though no federal legislation or court decision sanctions the change.

While the Supreme Court did rule that it was unconstitutional to deny federal financial benefits to same-sex couples on the same basis as other married couples, it explicitly refused to get involved in the more fundamental issue of the legality of same sex marriage. But, no matter, Obama and Holder were determined to move ahead anyway.

In February 2014, the Hill reported that "the Justice Department plans to issue a "policy memorandum which will allow same-sex couples to be able to file jointly for bankruptcy and will mandate that they will not be compelled to testify against each other in trial, among other new rights."[9]

Spousal privilege protects confidential communications between married couples and, in some cases, prevents them from testifying against each other. By extending marital privilege to same-sex couples, Obama is going much further in legalizing their marriages even when states — who solely control marriage law — have refused to do so.

Many conservatives have rightfully questioned how far Obama can go in using executive orders to shape America into his vision without the consent of our elected representatives in Congress.

Senator Mike Lee (R-UT) cited the standard legal test, first described by Supreme Court Justice Robert Jackson on the level of scrutiny to be given to the president's executive orders, which states:

> The president's authority to issue executive orders is strongest when he does so with the backing of Congress (category one), more dubious when he issues an order pertaining to a topic on which Congress has not passed a law (category two), and weakest when the executive order is 'incompatible with a congressional command' (category three).[10]

So how do Obama's executive actions comport with the Jackson test?

They flunk it!

Most of his executive orders either go expressly against what Congress enacted or implement policies and programs that Congress has considered and rejected. But no matter, Obama grabbed the power and reversed the will of the duly elected Congress. Consider these:

- Congress rejected the DREAM Act, yet Obama proceeded to implement it anyway.

- It rejected Cap and Trade (environmental emissions accountability programs), but the EPA imposed its own regulations, having the same effect as the statute.

- The House and the Senate have chosen not to pass bills reducing crack cocaine sentences retroactively, but Obama is using the pardon and clemency power to do it anyway.

- Despite the explicit language of the welfare reform and Affordable Care Act (ACA) statutes, delayed or canceled many of the ACA programs, overriding the clear meaning of the welfare reform law.

- Obama ignored the National Defense Authorization Act, which required a 30-day notice to Congress before the release of any of the terrorists detained at Guantanamo Bay, and, instead, released five of the top terrorists in exchange for American soldier Bowe Bergdahl.

With the executive branch free to legislate on its own and to change laws already in effect, we are straying ever further from the system of checks and balances built into our constitution.

POINT THREE: PACKING THE ELECTORATE

A key part of Obama's obsessive strategy to bring about one-party government is his resolve to lure solid Democratic Party voters into the electorate. Whether they are illegal immigrants or convicted felons, the presidential power grab provides something for each and every one of them, and is designed to reward them and gain their everlasting support.

Identity politics and ethnic voting are the essential building blocks in Obama's quest for one party control of American politics. Benefiting from the nearly unanimous vote of African-Americans for the Democratic Party, he hopes to create, among Latinos, the same kind of loyalty. And then, through immigration reform, he wants to increase their share of the American electorate even more rapidly than it otherwise would.

The Latino vote has increased exponentially in recent years and, even without immigration reform, is likely to continue to rise substantially.

Even in the short period between the elections of 2008 and 2012, the Latino vote rose by 1.4 million.[11] And the continued potential for a huge increase in the Hispanic vote, even among those who are already here, is enormous. While Hispanics are 17.2 percent of US population, and 15 percent of all adults, 11.2 percent of citizens, they are, at the moment, only 8.9 percent of actual voters.[12] That will likely change quickly.

Once African-Americans lagged badly in voter registration and participation, but no more. In 2012, 66.2 percent of eligible African-Americans voted — only slightly less than the white turnout of 64.1 percent.[13] Moreover, the population of Latinos in the United States is soaring. The Census Bureau estimates that the Hispanic population will rise from its current 17 percent of the US total to over 30 percent by 2050.[14]

Obama and the democrats hope that Latinos will continue to vote for them by top-heavy margins.

Between 1980 and 2012, the average Democratic margin of victory among Hispanic voters was 28 percent. Only in 2004, when Bush lost Latinos by "only" 58-40, did the Republican candidate even come close.

HISPANIC VOTE IN PRESIDENTIAL ELECTIONS 1980-2012[15]

Source: Pew Research Center

- **1980:** Carter, 56%; Reagan, 35%; Democratic Advantage +21
- **1984:** Mondale, 61%; Reagan, 37% ; Democratic Advantage +24
- **1988:** Dukakis, 69%; G.H.W. Bush, 30%; Democratic Advantage +39
- **1992:** Clinton, 61%; G.H.W. Bush, 25%; Democratic Advantage +36
- **1996:** Clinton, 72%; Dole, 21%; Democratic Advantage +51
- **2000:** Gore, 62%; G.W. Bush, 35%; Democratic Advantage +27
- **2004:** Kerry, 58%; G.W. Bush, 40%; Democratic Advantage +18
- **2008:** Obama, 67%; McCain, 31%; Democratic Advantage +36
- **2012:** Obama, 71%; Romney, 27%; Democratic Advantage +44

With about 13 percent of the national vote cast by African-Americans[16] (no significant increase in that population is forecast by the Census Bureau), it would seem that the Democratic Party has only to let immigration and time deliver them a permanent national majority.

But Obama isn't taking any chances. Many of his executive orders are directed straight at Latino voters.

OBAMA CUTS DEPORTATIONS WITHOUT APPROVAL OF CONGRESS

But Obama is determined not to wait. Using political advocacy and executive authority, he is breaking down the immigration barriers, one after the other.

OBAMA PASSES THE DREAM ACT BY EXECUTIVE ORDER

Part of Obama's political genius is his ability to break down controversial programs into their component parts to find an aspect of the issue that will elicit mass support among American voters.

For example, when it comes to abortion, he speaks of allowing for victims of rape or incest, taking the question to its extreme in the hopes of picking up support.

On the issue of immigration, Obama seized on the DREAM Act to promote his cause.

The DREAM Act, introduced in the Senate in 2001, provided for legal status and a path to citizenship for illegal immigrants who arrived in America when they were under age sixteen, brought here by their parents.

To be eligible, they had to have lived in the United States for at least five continuous years, and either graduated from high school or enlisted in the military. If they did, they would be able to become permanent legal residents, get a green card, and apply for full citizenship. They also had to be of "good moral character." (Whatever that means.) An estimated 800,000 children and young adults now in the United States meet these requirements.[17]

When the Democrats took over the House and the Senate in the elections of 2006, the DREAM Act seemed to have a good chance of passage and, after Obama's election, it seemed certain.

But the bill was defeated. It passed the House, but, without much Republican support, getting only fifty-five votes in the Senate, short of the sixty required for passage.

The DREAMers stayed in limbo until Obama was deep into his campaign for reelection. Facing criticism from Latinos for his failure to pass immigration reform, especially while he commanded sixty votes in the Senate, he hastily concocted an executive order to achieve the goals of the DREAM Act.

To hell with Congress; he would do it by executive order — by the stroke of his pen! On June 15, 2012 — four and a half months before the election — he ordered his administration to stop deporting illegal immigrants who would have qualified under the DREAM Act.

Under his order, people under age thirty who came to the United States before the age of sixteen, have no criminal record, have been living here for five consecutive years, and who are in school or the military can get a two-year immunity from deportation and apply for work permits.

In effect, Obama was announcing that he would not enforce the existing immigration law when it came to the DREAMers.

Obama's power grab had the desired effect. The order sent an electric shock through the Latino community. Overnight, Obama acquired a popularity he had lacked before.

His poll ratings among Latinos soared. In the end, he defeated Romney among Hispanics by 71–27; while in running against McCain, he had scored better with Hispanics by only 67–31.

Was his deferral of deportations of young Latinos legal? No. Although the president has broad discretion in prioritizing law enforcement, he cannot simply will away our laws by fiat.

Obama clearly had no legal authority to grant the DREAM Act kids legal status or work permits since these instruments are regulated by law. Even the president cannot change the status of someone from illegal to legal simply by the stroke of a pen or the wink of an eye.

Congressman Tom Rice (R-SC) tried to fight back and introduced a resolution asking for the House of Representatives to sue the administration for reversing an act of Congress in the DREAM Act order. Whether the House will, indeed, sue or whether the courts will agree, is up in the air.

But what is clear is that Obama got away with it. His power grab worked — add 800,000 to the permanent democratic voter tally!

Now he moves onto his greater goal: The enfranchisement of more than ten million currently illegal immigrants. Pushing hard for legalization in Congress, the left is determined to get the vote of these potential Democrats.

Republicans are willing to consider legalizing their work status but are understandably reluctant to let them become citizens and block vote for Democrats. Republicans are also pressing for measures to seal the southern border and stop further illegal immigration. Some, like Senator John Cornyn (R-TX), are pushing an amendment to the immigration bill requiring that the border be effectively sealed before any legalization can take place. Without that, they say, there is an incentive for millions more to come in illegally and wait their turn for amnesty in the future. The real solution seems to be to separate legalized work status from citizenship and voting. Many Republicans say it is fine to let illegal immigrants stay here and work if they commit no crimes, but that they would have to go back to their native lands and wait on the end of the line for legal status to be able to become citizens here and vote.

As immigration reform stalls in Congress, Obama is once again resorting to his old habit of reform by executive order. He may not be able to legalize those who are not here legally (although he is trying in the DREAM Act), but he can stop them from being deported. In 2012, the United States deported 409,000 illegal immigrants.[18]

But, in 2013 — as the immigration bill ran into Republican opposition in the House — Obama curtailed the deportation rate dramatically. *The Washington Times* reported that "authorities deported fewer illegal immigrants in fiscal 2013 than at any time since President Obama took office, according to secret numbers obtained by the Center for Immigration Studies that suggest Mr. Obama's non-deportation policies have hindered removals."[19] Only 364,000 were removed in the year, a drop of 11 percent from 2012.[20]

Indeed, Alabama Republican Senator Jeff Sessions reported that a study of the deportation cases in 2013 indicates that 98 percent of those sent away from our borders were either caught red-handed sneaking in, had been convicted of crimes other than immigration offenses while in the United States, or had already been deported and returned.[21] In other words, fewer than 10,000 illegal immigrants were deported just for being here. If they did not commit a crime while here, Obama left them alone, bringing a virtual halt to the battle against illegal immigration. And it looks like Obama wants to cut the deportation rates even further. On March 14, 2014, he ordered a review of deportation practices demanding that the Department of Homeland Security act "more humanely within the context of the law."[22]

Acting in response to Latino pressure to reduce deportations, the president ordered the DHS to prepare an "inventory" of deportation practices so he can cut and prune where he wishes. All along, Obama has maintained that he does not have the authority to stop deportations, although he did exactly that when he allowed DREAM kids to stay and avoid being sent back to their parents' native countries. *The Los Angeles Times* reported that President Obama "emphasized his deep concern about the pain too many families feel from the separation that comes from our broken immigration system."[23] These concerns will likely lead him to keep even more illegal immigrants in the United States, contrary to American laws.

Already, he has cut fines imposed on companies that hire illegal immigrants, thus reducing the most effective sanction the law offers to cut the flow of undocumented workers into the United States. *The Washington Times* reports that the Obama administration has begun to cut "a break for businesses that violate immigration hiring rules, reducing their fines by an average of 40 percent from what they should be, according to an audit by the Homeland Security Inspector General. One business saw its fine cut from $4.9 million to slightly more than $1 million, a 78 percent drop."[24] The Inspector General noted that, "the knowledge that fines can be significantly reduced may diminish the effectiveness of fines as a deterrent to hiring unauthorized workers."[25]

OBAMA AND HOLDER TRY TO GIVE EX-FELONS THE VOTE

By hook or crook, Obama remains determined to expand the voting rolls to include as many currently illegal immigrants as possible, confident that his party can win their votes far into the future. He'll do it any way he can — new laws, non-enforcement of current laws, or executive orders. He won't give up.

Attorney General Eric Holder has even found another way to expand the electorate to include a lot of new democratic voters: Give convicted felons the right to vote.

Currently, four states — Florida, Kentucky, Iowa, and Virginia — do not allow anyone who has been convicted of a felony to vote. Some other states let them vote once they get out of prison. Others allow them the ballot once their paroles are over and, for others, they have to clear probation as well. Still others impose a waiting period before a person convicted of a felony can cast a vote. But it has apparently not escaped Holder's notice that three of the seven key swing states in the nation — Florida, Iowa, and Virginia — all ban anyone convicted of a felony from ever casting a ballot again.

Letting released felons vote would significantly skew the electoral process in favor of the Democrats. Of the 5.8 million felons who cannot vote, one-third are African-Americans. In 2002, researchers at the University of Minnesota and Northwestern University said that the 2000 presidential election "would almost certainly have been reversed" had felons been permitted to vote in Florida.[26]

Holder describes the ban on felons voting as a vestige of the racist policies of the South after the Civil War noting that "those swept up in the system often had their rights rescinded, their dignity diminished, and the full measure of their citizenship revoked for the rest of their lives. They could not vote."[27] By framing the issue as a racial question, Holder is trying to appeal to liberal sympathies. But the denial of the right to vote to felons cuts across sectional lines. It's not like there has been a grassroots clamor to retire voting rights for convicted felons. Only two states — Maine and Vermont — let felons vote while they are in prison (by absentee ballot). Thirteen others let them vote as soon as they are released. (Hawaii, Illinois, Indiana, Massachusetts, Michigan, Montana, New Hampshire, North Dakota, Ohio, Oregon, Pennsylvania, Rhode Island, and Utah). All others have restrictions on felon voting. Such clearly non-racist states as California, New York, Connecticut, and Colorado, for example, permit them the ballot only after they have cleared parole.

The largest group (twenty states) let them vote after they have cleared both parole and probation. These include non-southern states like Idaho, Kansas, Alaska, Maryland, Minnesota, Missouri, Nebraska, New Jersey, New Mexico, South Dakota, Washington state, and Wisconsin.

So Holder is being disingenuous when he says felons cannot vote because many of them are black. The Supreme Court has upheld bans on felon voting. In 1974, in *Richardson v. Ramirez* the court ruled that the ban was explicitly allowed under the Fourteenth Amendment, passed after the Civil War, which had denied that right to former Confederates. Mindful that the ban on letting former felons vote might be used for racial segregation, the court held that if the enforcement of the ban was racially discriminatory, it could be overturned. But a law that made no distinction based on race was valid, the Court held.[28]

Now, Holder is saying that denying felons the vote has a "disparate impact" on blacks since African-American men are only 7 percent of the population, but an estimated one-third of those disenfranchised by the law.[29]

It seems not to have occurred to Holder that states do not want those who flouted their laws to determine who writes them. A state's desire to exclude those who have committed serious crimes from voting, at least while serving their sentence (which includes parole and probation) does not seem unreasonable except to those casting about for a way to carry Florida, Iowa, and Virginia in elections.

Holder is clearly intent on aiding Obama in using the excuse of discrimination to increase the democratic vote in swing states.

Sometimes these contaminated voter rolls can play a huge role in our national politics. After the elections of 2008, the democratic drive to win a sixty vote supermajority in the Senate hinged on the contest in Minnesota in which Republican incumbent Norm Coleman faced democratic challenger Al Franken. On election night, news reports showed Coleman was winning by over 700 votes. But the recounts and reviews conducted by the largely democratic canvassing board and courts whittled the margin down until Franken was declared the winner by 312 votes.

An investigation by a conservative watchdog group, the Minnesota Majority, found that "at least 341 convicted felons in largely democratic Minneapolis-St. Paul voted illegally" in the contest, more than enough to offset Franken's margin of victory even after election officials had monkeyed with the results.[30]

There's more. Obama's got more ideas to bring convicted felons into the Democratic Party fold. While Holder works to give felons the right to vote, Obama's Equal Employment Opportunity Commission (EEOC) has ruled that the use of criminal background checks in hiring is racially discriminatory. You heard it right. Arrest records cannot be used as the basis for a decision not to hire, to fire, or to suspend an employee. According to the EEOC, arrest records are unreliable. Although an employer can order a criminal background check, it must provide notice to the potential employee, provide them with a copy, and permit them to comment on the report. In 2012, it issued "guidance" to businesses. Noting that since blacks and Hispanics are convicted of crimes at significantly higher rates than whites, the EEOC ruled that refusing to hire job applicants based on their criminal records would have "a disparate impact based on race and national origin."[31+]

"Disparate impact" is the constitutional law theory that holds that even if a policy is not intended to be discriminatory, if it affects one or more protected groups disproportionately, it is impermissible.

The EEOC doesn't explicitly say that you cannot refuse to hire a felon because of his criminal record, but it does require that businesses "effectively link specific criminal conduct, and its dangers, with the risks inherent in the duties of a particular position."[32] So let's see. If a business wants to hire a bookkeeper, can the business deny an applicant who was convicted for insurance fraud? Is the fact that the business doesn't engage in insurance enough to remove the insurance fraud from consideration? How about a conviction for assault? Wouldn't most employers be concerned about hiring someone with any kind of violent conviction, regardless of what the job is? But could a fast food employer be investigated and fined for refusing to hire an offender with a history of violence? And here's an even more basic problem. Almost all criminal convictions are the result of plea bargains. Indeed, 97 percent of state convictions and 94 percent of federal convictions are based on plea bargain in which the defendant pleads guilty to a crime that is considerably lesser in seriousness that the one originally charged.[33]

The questions go on and on, but the Obama appointed EEOC is way out there on this issue.

Employers who cannot prove to the EEOC's satisfaction that excluding a felon from a particular job is a "business necessity" could face discrimination charges.[34] Amplifying the EEOC policy, Commissioner Victoria Lipnic warned employers, in a speech before the US Chamber of Commerce in March 2012, that one "bright-line policy you should not adopt is having a no-felons policy. If you have that policy, that's going to be a problem if you're subject to an EEOC investigation."[35] The world is turning upside down. Felons may get the right to vote and businesses may lose the right to refuse them employment.

It is all part of Obama's power grab; his plan for one-party governance in America.

Point Four: Protecting and Encouraging Voter Fraud

If Obama cannot expand the electorate as rapidly as he would like, he can use the powers of his office to allow his allies to engage in massive voter fraud, stuff ballot boxes, and vote multiple times and get away with it. The Democrats under Obama have refined voter fraud to an art form. For his part, Obama and Attorney General Eric Holder have done all they can to stop photo identification to be required before a vote can be cast. They say this is to enhance turnout of minority voters, but it is really a device to shield voter fraud from detection.

As the partisan divide in America sharpens and the two parties compete with relatively equal strength, the potential of fraud to influence the outcome of elections looms ever greater. The battle over who won Florida in the 2000 elections presaged a decade of close races, often decided by the fiat of those who count the ballots. Remember what Stalin said: "It's not the people who vote that count, it's the people who count the votes."[36]

Allegations of voter fraud are often partisan based on whose side you're on. But the impartial, respected, and nonpartisan Pew Research Foundation's Center on the States highlights certain uncontested facts:

- Approximately 24 million voter registrations in the United States are no longer valid or are significantly inaccurate.

- More than 1.8 million deceased individuals are listed as voters.

- Approximately 2.75 million people have registrations in more than one state.[37]

In key states, True The Vote, a nonpartisan voter-integrity group, found 348,000 deceased individuals[38] still on the voter rolls. Some of the states with the largest number of deceased registered voters are:

- California: 49,000
- Florida: 30,000
- Texas: 28,500
- Michigan: 25,000
- Illinois: 24,000[39]

Ohio's Secretary of State — the chief election official — has found that in Morrow and Wood Counties, there are more registered voters than residents. He says that he wants to purge the voter rolls of ineligible voters, but that federal regulations make that very difficult. Under the provisions of the 1993 National Voter Registration Act (NVRA), he can only remove voter names from the rolls if a person is deceased, is an ineligible felon, or has either confirmed a change of address or requested to have their registration canceled. "As a result," he says, "Ohio's county boards of elections must wait years to remove potentially ineligible voters, even in circumstances where the evidence suggests these individuals have moved and should not be eligible."[40]

The inefficiency — or legal inability — of the states in maintaining proper voting rolls leaves a huge potential for partisan abuse.

A decade ago, Kansas' prescient secretary of state Kris Kobach initiated an arrangement with other state election officials to swap voter information to see how many people double voted. By the 2012 elections, twenty-seven states participated in the study. North Carolina compared those who had voted there with people who cast ballots in other states. The election officials looked for people who voted in North Carolina and had the same first and last names and birth dates as those who had voted in other states. They identified 35,000 people who appear to have voted in two states — not just registered in two places, but actually voted twice!!! In over 700 cases, the voters had the same Social Security numbers too![41]

In 2012, Romney carried North Carolina by over 100,000 votes, so the fraud did not affect the outcome. But, in 2008, Obama carried it by 13,000, so had the double voting occurred then, it could have influenced the results.

OBAMA ADMINISTRATION FIGHTS PHOTO ID LAWS

To counter voter fraud, states have sought to require photo identification in order to vote. Relatively foolproof, photo IDs would effectively stop double voting and make it unlikely that ineligible people could vote.

But here again, the Obama administration has fought against these measures tooth and nail, litigating up to the US Supreme Court to stop them. The argument it makes is that requiring photo identification would have a chilling effect on the electoral process and deter many people from voting. They point out that large numbers of poor and downscale voters do not have drivers' licenses or passports and do not want to pay the fee necessary to obtain them.

Some states, like Texas and Pennsylvania, have countered by providing free photo IDs to anyone who requests them, often distributed at motor vehicle bureau offices throughout their states. There's an easy way to solve this. States should automatically provide photo identification whenever someone registers to vote, just as they do when they issue drivers licenses. Such a program would quickly end much of the potential for voter fraud. So far, Georgia, Indiana, Kansas, Tennessee, Florida, and Texas have photo ID laws in effect. Arkansas, Mississippi, North Carolina, Virginia, Pennsylvania, and Wisconsin have passed photo ID laws but they are not yet in effect pending judicial challenges.

Can it be mere coincidence that the Justice Department has litigated against photo ID laws in the swing states of North Carolina, Virginia, Pennsylvania, and Wisconsin? The ferocity of the Justice Department challenges to photo ID laws substantiates the charge that the Obama administration seeks to encourage voter fraud to prop up its majorities. With photo identification readily available for free, only a desire to encourage unregistered or even non-citizens to vote illegally could account for such passionate opposition to photo ID laws.

The Richardson family of Cincinnati gives us a real life glimpse into voter fraud. Channel 9 describes how county documents show that Mrs. Richardson cast an absentee ballot on November 1, 2012. She also voted at a precinct because, in her patriotic zeal, she was "afraid her absentee ballot would not be counted in time." Her granddaughter, India Richardson celebrated her first-ever ballot by casting a second one as well.[42]

The growing use of absentee ballots and the increasing prevalence of early voting maximize the opportunities for fraud. Thirty-two million votes were cast early or as absentee ballots in the election of 2012 — a quarter of all the votes that year.[43] In some swing states like Florida (53 percent) and Ohio (31 percent), the total was even higher.

Early or absentee voting erodes the protections of the secret ballot. Reports are rife that groups like ACORN (the Association of Community Organizations for Reform Now) canvass nursing homes, Indian reservations, welfare offices and the like with forms for absentee voting where downscale and elderly voters mark their ballots with their friendly ACORN representative looking over their shoulders.

A study of early voting in Ohio by the University of Akron found that those who cast ballots before Election Day were more likely to be Democrats. In the state's gubernatorial election of 2010, for example, Election Day voters supported the Republican, John Kasich (the winner), by 51–48, while early voters backed the Democrat by 53–47.[44]

Democratic Party tactics increasingly emphasize getting out the early vote. Their efforts focus on low income and minority votes, more likely to back their candidates. In the Ohio study, 43 percent of early voters in 2010 had incomes of less than $35,000 a year compared with only 23 percent of those who voted on Election Day.[45]

Photo IDs are necessary to combat this rampant voter fraud. If costs are not an issue, there is no legitimate argument against voter IDs. Think about it: What is the big deal about showing a photo ID? Every person traveling on a plane or train in the United States must routinely show a photo ID. We do it all the time. Is that so traumatic?

Many private office buildings in large cities require photo IDs. So do storage facilities and banks. Even some department stores require a photo ID before a valid credit card is accepted. So, showing a photo ID before voting would not be some barbarian practice that violated the privacy or civil liberties of the prospective voter. What possible, legitimate objection is there to this proposal?

The objection can only be based on a fear of uncovering fraud.

THE BLACK PANTHER PARTY INTIMIDATES WHITE VOTERS AND JUSTICE DEPARTMENT DROPS THE CASE

Obama and Holder are not so quick to pounce on instances of intimidation of white voters. On Election Day, 2008, two members of the Black Panther Party, Minister King Samir Shabazz and Jerry Jackson, stood outside the entrance to a Philadelphia polling station, threatening and taunting white voters. Both were dressed in paramilitary uniforms and Shabazz carried a billy club which he pointed at white voters while both men shouted racial slurs including "white devil" and "you're about to be ruled by the black man, cracker."[46] The police sent Shabazz away but let Jackson stay since he was a certified poll watcher. The incident was caught on tape by a bystander and circulated over YouTube.

The Justice Department investigated and, with two weeks left in Bush's term, brought a civil suit against Minister King Samir Shabazz, Jerry Jackson, National Black Party Panther chairman Malik Zulu Shabazz, and the Black Panther Party itself. The lawsuit accused them of using uniforms, racial insults, and a weapon to intimidate voters and those who were there to assist them. The case remained open when the Obama administration took office a few weeks later.

In April 2009, Bartie Bull, a former civil rights lawyer who was serving as a poll watcher at the polling station where the incident occurred, submitted an affidavit at justice's request supporting the lawsuit, stating that he considered it to have been the most severe instance of voter intimidation he had ever encountered.[47] None of the defendants who were charged appeared in court to answer the charges and career attorneys at the Justice Department assumed a default judgment would be entered against the Panthers. But the Justice Department was now ruled by Eric Holder and the efforts of the career attorneys to pursue a default judgment were overruled by two of their line superiors, acting Assistant Attorney General Loretta King and acting Deputy Assistant Attorney General Steve Rosenbaum. Instead of getting a default judgment, the Justice Department dismissed all charges against the New Black Panther Party and Jerry Jackson and narrowed the charges against Minister King Shabazz. Career attorney J. Christian Adams resigned from the Department in protest.

The United States Civil Rights Commission challenged the Justice Department's dismissal of the case saying "though it had basically won the case, the Civil Rights Division took the unusual move of voluntarily dismissing the charges. The division's public rationale would send the wrong message entirely — that attempts at voter suppression will be tolerated and will not be vigorously prosecuted so long as the groups or individuals who engage in them fail to respond to the charges leveled against them."[48]

By using fraud, intimidation, double voting, and ballot irregularities, President Obama and Attorney General Holder are making a mockery of fair and free elections in the United States.

And by fabricating the ridiculous myth that getting a photo ID is so burdensome that it will discourage minority turnout, they are allowing the fraud to go on.

It's another big power grab designed to assure a one party government.

Point Five: Intimidating Republicans and Conservatives

Part of the effort to build a permanent, one-party government must, by definition, include a plan to emasculate and destroy the Republican Party and conservative movement and discredit outspoken critics of Obama. Like Richard Nixon, Obama has an "enemies list." And he's out to get them.

He's tried to keep it secret, but sometimes the Obama administration's clumsy machinations come to light and the naked power grab is right in front of us, impossible to ignore.

The efforts of President Obama and his supporters to intimidate and silence their opponents rarely involve anything as blatant as Black Panther billy clubs, but its effect is equally paralyzing. President Obama's weapon of choice has been his Internal Revenue Service, which he has used to intimidate and marginalize his political foes and is especially targeted at the Republican Party — the entire Republican Party.

He has used to it pointedly to cripple the Tea Party movement, which was largely responsible for defeating his congressional allies in the elections of 2010. That same year, in the case of *Citizens United v. FEC*, the US Supreme Court had the temerity to strike down the provisions of the federal election law that restricted independent expenditures for political advocacy by corporations, associations, or labor unions.

President Obama was so outraged, that he took the unprecedented and undignified step of attacking the decision from the podium during his 2010 State of the Union speech, with the Supreme Court Justices sitting right in the front row, unable to respond. His petty animosity was on display.

No sooner had the Court ruled than the Obama administration went to work using the executive power of the IRS to nullify the effect of the *Citizens United* decision. Behind closed doors, the IRS began to identify the enemy conservative and non-profit organizations and start slow-walking their applications for tax-exempt status to take advantage of the decision.

Obama allies, like brash New York Democratic Senator Chuck Schumer, shamelessly called for a constitutional amendment to reverse the *Citizens United* decision,[49] claiming it was "the worst decision since *Plessy v. Ferguson*.[50] Schumer, along with Democratic Senators Michael Bennet, Sheldon Whitehouse, Jeff Merkley, Tom Udall, Jeanne Shaheen, and Al Franken, tried to pressure the IRS and signed a joint letter asking for regulations to restrict the fundraising by the Tea Party and similar groups.[51] According to TheBlaze.com, Schumer urged the Obama administration to circumvent Congress and adopt new rules targeted at troublesome conservative groups through the IRS.[52] The Senator continued, "But there are many things that can be done administratively by the IRS and other government agencies — we must redouble those efforts immediately."[53]

Much remains to be learned about the genesis of this campaign of harassment. Congressman David Camp, Chairman of the House Ways and Means Committee investigating the matter said that "there continues to be an ongoing investigation, with many documents yet to be uncovered, into how the IRS systematically targeted and abused conservative-leaning groups,"[54]

Congressional hearings have yet to uncover a smoking gun linking the president personally to the efforts of the IRS to threaten, harass, and weaken his political opponents, but such specific evidence would only be necessary for impeachment, which is highly unlikely in any event. But for us to understand the power grab that is really going on, the evidence doesn't have to rise to that level.

It is abundantly clear, from the testimony and documents amassed by the House Government Oversight Committee hearings, that a group of IRS agents, members of the left-wing political activist union that represents all Treasury Department employees, subjected The Tea Party and other conservative activists to extraordinary scrutiny and deliberate delays in processing their applications for status as tax-exempt political groups. While they processed similar applications from liberal organizations with speed and only superficial investigation, conservative groups had to wait two to three years to get approval. They were dogged by requests for information that were staggering in their complexity and posed serious administrative burdens for the citizen groups that had scant financial or staffing resources to use in meeting them.

One note about "tax-exempt" status: Donations to 501(c)(4) groups like the Tea Party are taxable. There is no tax deduction that comes with the donation. Funds given to these organizations are strictly after-tax money.

The tax exemption in question only applies to the organization itself. Jenny Beth Martin, founder and head of the Tea Party Patriots, the largest of the Tea Party groups, explains why they need the tax exemption: "As a 501(c)(4)," she explains, "we don't have tax exemptions for donations. We rely on small donors, which is why being designated as a non-profit is so important. To raise money by phone and mail we need the non-profit status to comply with postal requirements for nonprofit mailing status and state requirements for phone calls which solicit donations."[55]

If the IRS refused to grant a tax exemption to any citizen group like the Tea Party, they would owe the government a corporate income tax on all of the funds they raise. And, since none of the groups have been paying taxes while they waited for their anticipated tax exemptions to come through, they would owe back taxes dating to their founding in 2009 — a burden that would simply wipe them out of existence, the unquestionable goal of the IRS and the Obama Administration.

The experience of one of the groups applying for tax-exempt status illustrates the extreme measures that the Obama administration engaged in to bury them in paperwork and outrageous administrative demands. Like the Southern literacy tests of old that were used to keep African Americans from voting, the IRS made the groups spend years of administrative time to request tax- exempt status. The IRS asked this group seeking a 501(c)(4) designation to respond to 124 separate questions, each requiring a substantial amount of research, including:

- What are your activities for the coming year?

- Attach copies of brochures, pamphlets, newsletters, fliers, advertisements or any literature you have issued.

- Will you offer classes, workshops or lectures? If so, covering what? Submit sample of materials used. How will fees be determined? How much of your gross receipts will come from these? How many staff will be allocated? Will you pay honoraria?

- Who selects materials for your website? On what criteria? Is it free? Is it copyright-ed? Who controls the data? Do you sell ads? What are annual gross receipts? Will you sell products on line? Please explain in detail.

- Will you conduct rallies for or against any public legislation or candidates? Time and location of each rally, copy of each handout, names of people in your organization and their compensation and time on the rallies, what percent of your time will be spent on these? What expenses?

- Explain the nature and extent of lobbying, staff time.

- Have any candidates addressed your group? Who? When? What materials? Attach video or audio recordings, if any.

- Have you worked with any other group? Give details, cost, staffing, percent of time.

- Do you conduct voter registration or "get-out-the-vote" drives? Time and location? On whose behalf? Submit all printed materials. What percent of time and staff and money will you spend on it?

- Will you use an officer's personal residence for your work? Details? Cost?

- Provide all leases, contracts, rentals, loan or financing agreements.

- How do you solicit funds? Send copies of all solicitations, brochures etc. Fundraising costs? What percent of staff and budget on fund raising?

- Financial statements 2007-2011. Breakdown of income and spending.

- What employees? For each: title, duties, pay.

- Resumes of all directors and officers — Any involvement in litigation? Explain?[56]

And remember, as you look over these voluminous questions, that 501(c)(4) organizations are legally allowed to spend as much time as they want lobbying on legislation, so long as it pertains to their core purpose. Advocacy is totally permissible and it can spend money on partisan campaigns as long as they constitute less than half of its work.

Note that the IRS examiners were careful to request the donor lists of conservative groups. An investigation by the House Oversight Committee found that the IRS used these donor lists to target individuals for tax audits. The Republicans on the House Ways and Means Committee found that 10 percent of the Tea Party donors were audited compared to 1 percent of the general population.[57]

But Obama did not stop at harassing conservative groups with an IRS inquisition. He has recently moved to exterminate them. On the day after Thanksgiving in 2013 — when the media was least likely to cover it — the IRS went a big step further in penalizing conservative speech and issued proposed regulations that essentially blocked all political activity by tax-exempt groups entirely. In weighing the balance between political activity and social welfare advocacy, the IRS put its thumb on the scale and designated almost all forms of public action as political, virtually assuring that the groups would have a choice of saying nothing or losing their tax exemption.

Rob Boysen, the coordinator of the Tea Party Patriots for Eastern Pennsylvania, explained how the new regulations "will stifle political speech and make it more difficult for citizen-led groups and associations to effectively function."[58]

He says that the new rules effectively "codify" the targeting of conservative groups by IRS audits. He called them "a blatant attempt to legalize the illegal discrimination and oppression of American citizens' right to freedom of speech — particularly political speech — that is guaranteed by the First Amendment."[59] The new rules would redefine political activity so as to make it practically impossible to conduct "voter registration activities, host forums or debates with our representatives in Washington, publish voter guides and voting records and to even mention the names of elected officials in public statements."[60] FOX News reported that the new rules "curtail activities such as running ads, distributing campaign literature and other get-out-the-vote activities."[61]

While the ruling applies to groups supporting both parties, it mainly serves to hurt the president's opponents, since labor unions have many other ways of influencing elections. The new Thanksgiving Day IRS proposed ruling effectively neutralizes the ability of conservative groups to speak out politically and reverses the *Citizens United* decision that affirmatively allowed it.

Congressman Dave Camp, Chairman of the House Ways and Means Committee was skeptical of the IRS ruling, claiming that "[the ruling of the administration] smacks of trying to shut down potential critics." He said that the new rules were "drafted in a manner, in my view, to shut down tea party groups."[62]

The American Center for Law and Justice (ACLJ) is representing forty-one organizations in a federal lawsuit challenging the IRS for its wrong-doing in politically-based targeting of conservative and Tea Party groups. Their attorney, Jay Sekulow, said he wants "to hold those responsible for the unlawful targeting scheme accountable for their actions." He warns that "the Obama Administration is determined to further limit the free speech of Americans by attempting to change constitutional practices that are decades old."[63]

The IRS claimed that the new Thanksgiving rule would clarify the status of 501(c)(4) advocacy groups and end confusion about their status. But when Congress subpoenaed e-mails from IRS and Treasury officials, it turned out that the rules had been conceived by the very IRS official who was in charge of the harassment of conservative groups – Lois Lerner. Working in tandem with officials of the Treasury Department during the 2012 election, she plotted to muzzle conservative groups completely with the new rules during Obama's second term. (When Lerner was asked about the IRS' activity before a congressional committee, she took the Fifth Amendment.)

IRS officials who worked with Lerner called their work "off-plan," meaning that it would not be published in any public record prior to the election. Congressman Camp attacked the off-the-record drafting of the new rules saying, "If Treasury and the IRS fabricated the rationale for a rule change it would tend to raise questions about the integrity of the rule-making."[64]

IRS HARASSES NON-POLITICAL GROUP OF
CONSERVATIVE ENTERTAINERS

Sometimes the IRS goes after groups that are not involved in political campaigning — just because they are conservative.

A group of 1,700 actors, producers, writers, directors, and studio execs in Hollywood set up a social organization called Friends of Abe [Lincoln]. Its director, Jeremy Boreing, says that the group "has absolutely no political agenda. It exists to create fellowship among like-minded individuals."[65] It includes among its members actors Jon Voight, Gary Sinise, and Kelsey Grammer. One can easily understand that conservatives in Hollywood could use some fellowship with like-minded individuals.

But the IRS has been on its case for three years deciding whether or not to grant it tax-exempt status. The political thought police at the IRS raised their eyebrows when the group invited Herman Cain and Paul Ryan to speak. The sticking point is that the IRS wants the membership list of the organization and Friends of Abe doesn't want to — and shouldn't have to — share their membership list. Fears of a blacklist against its members haunt the group as they seek to thrive in a left-wing town on the "Left" Coast.

There is no legitimate purpose in harassing Friends of Abe since it has no politically activist inclinations, but the IRS is doing it anyway.

IRS TARGETS DELAWARE REPUBLICAN SENATE CANDIDATE
CHRISTINE O'DONNELL

Even more chilling than proceeding against conservative groups is the apparent IRS effort to target Republican candidates. Many who run on the GOP label find themselves the objects of IRS audits right as they are announcing their candidacies. Were they going to be audited anyway? They never know. But one never hears any complaints about Democratic Party candidates who were audited once they became candidates.

The most blatant example was the IRS actions to derail Christine O'Donnell, the Republican candidate for Senate in Delaware in 2010. O'Donnell, who had the strong backing of the Tea Party, was embarrassed on the very day she announced her candidacy by a claim that she owed a federal tax lien of $11,733. It turned out that the lien was affixed to a house she had once owned but no longer did. The IRS eventually admitted the error and blamed it on a computer glitch.[66] But the damage to her credibility was enormous and was never repaired.

Ms. O'Donnell's suspicions about the origin of the leak of her confidential tax in-formation were aroused when she got a phone message, two years later, from a US Treasury Department agent warning that her private tax records may have been breached.

Two years later? It took them that long to figure it out!

The Washington Times reported the text of the phone message: Mrs. O'Donnell, this is Dennis Martel, special agent with the US Department of Treasury in Baltimore, MD . . . We received information that your personal federal tax info may have been compromised and may have been misused by an individual."[67] Martel told O'Donnell that an official in Delaware state government had improperly accessed her records on the same day as she announced her candidacy for the Senate.

After prodding by Senator Chuck Grassley (R-IA), the Delaware Director of Revenue, Patrick Carter, admitted that his agency accessed the federal tax records of an unnamed taxpayer. Because the access took place on March 20, 2010, just as O'Donnell was announcing her candidacy, reporters have naturally concluded that she was the taxpayer in question.[68] Carter acknowledged that he spoke to a federal Treasury Department investigator in December 2012 "about state investigator access of federal tax records."[69] Carter identified the Delaware official who pried into O'Donnell's tax records on the day she announced her candidacy as David Smith, an investigator for the department. Carter conceded that he was the one who approved the investigation.

Defending the accessing of her records (without ever admitting it was she who was targeted), Carter said his division "routinely compares state and federal tax records for discrepancies and potential investigation based on information provided on tax forms, financial information from other state government agencies, from tips or complaints, or from media coverage or other public information highlighting tax issues."[70] Carter was apparently referring to a news story in a Delaware paper based on a bogus tax lien leaked by the IRS.

Senator Grassley (R- IA) commented: "The State of Delaware looked at Ms. O'Donnell's federal records because of a newspaper article describing a federal tax lien against her. Does the state look at every taxpayer who faces a federal lien or only those who happen to appear in a newspaper article? Is it routine for a state employee to e-mail his boss about looking at a taxpayer's records on a Saturday, when the article appeared?"[71]

The Washington Times reports that "House Oversight Committee Chairman Darrell E. Issa (R-CA) said he's baffled that the Justice Department declined to prosecute a government employee who apparently knowingly pried into tax records of a political candidate or donor, and [Issa] said there should be a way for victims to know their rights have been violated."[72] The furor surrounding the release of the bogus tax lien at the time of O'Donnell's announcement of her Senate candidacy and the subsequent revelations that the state had accessed her tax information, led two chairmen of the most powerful committees in Congress: House Ways and Means Committee Chairman Dave Camp (R-MI) and Senate Finance Committee Chairman Max Baucus (D-MT) to investigate. But, outrageously, they will have to keep whatever they find out to themselves. Neither other members of Congress, nor the public, nor even O'Donnell herself can ever know who at the IRS was responsible.

Why not? Amazingly, federal law shields the disclosure of any such information. *The Washington Times* reports that "even Ms.

O'Donnell herself will not be briefed on what either congressional committee discovers, as the federal government asserts that tax law goes so far as to shield its own employees from being exposed publicly if they are engaged in willful targeting or other wrongdoing,"[73] *The Times* reports, adding that the only two people legally privy to the information are the chairmen of the investigating committees, Camp and Baucus. And they are not permitted to reveal what they learn.[74]

All of this evidence begs the question of how Smith got access, on Carter's orders to O'Donnell's tax return. It appears that Smith was a member of a special task force set up to hunt for tax delinquency. A source close to the investigation says that his service on the task force gave him access to the database. But, the source also notes, that without probable cause, he had no way to legally access O'Donnell's return. And, since she told investigators that neither he nor anyone in the Department of Finance or the IRS suspected her of criminal activity, he had no probable cause. It looks like the law that was intended to protect the privacy of taxpayers is really only used to protect the privacy of public officials who illegally access taxpayer records.

AND O'DONNELL IS NOT THE ONLY ONE

Not by a long shot. The US Treasury Inspector General for Tax Administration J. Russell George, told Iowa Republican Senator Chuck Grassley that he had turned up four cases in which unidentified government officials took part in "unauthorized access or disclosure of tax records of political donors or candidates."[75] Unfortunately, the Justice Department has declined to prosecute any of the violators.

The National Organization for Marriage, a group organized in 2008 to fight pro-gay marriage initiatives on ballots throughout the country, is suing the IRS, claiming it has evidence that someone within the agency leaked the organization's private donor list to its political enemies in 2012, but, not surprisingly, nobody has been held responsible. The organization's attorney, Cleta Mitchell, said that, "somebody did this deliberately [accessed its donor list and leaked it to its opponents] and we need to know who it was."[76]

John C. Eastman, chairman of the National Organization for Marriage, said the leaked forms bore internal IRS markings that someone tried to blur in the electronic document, indicating that they were trying to hide the origin. The information ended up in the hands of the Human Rights Campaign, a leading gay-rights group that is politically opposed to the National Organization for Marriage. Eastman, a law professor at Chapman University, told *The Washington Times* that this pattern "suggests to me that this this thing was deliberate and at high levels of the division, a political appointee, somebody. And darn it, we're going to find out who did it, and we're going to wrap it up with a bow and send it over to the Justice Department and keep the pressure on."[77]

After the donor list was leaked to the Human Rights Campaign, they posted it online. *The Huffington Post* revealed that the donations to the anti-same-sex marriage group included a $10,000 gift from a political action committee associated with Mitt Romney.

In both O'Donnell's case and that of the National Association for Marriage, the IRS told the groups and their attorneys that the identity of the IRS official who leaked the info cannot be released because that would mean disclosing confidential taxpayer information — even though they were the targets of the wrongdoing.

Does that make any sense at all?

Indeed, a source close to the O'Donnell investigation says that he has credible evidence of nine candidates or major campaign donors who "had their tax records inappropriately or illegally accessed and some disclosed to third parties."[78]

The IRS has also gone out of its way to target prominent donors to Republican and conservative causes. Most notable is the case of Sheldon Adelson, the billionaire owner of the Venetian Resort Hotel Casino and the Sands Expo and Convention Center, both in Las Vegas, Nevada. Adelson, reputed to be the fifth richest man in the United States with a fortune upwards of $40 billion, is a strong supporter of conservative causes. Adelson attracted attention when he said he was donating $10 million to the presidential campaign of Republican Newt Gingrich. His long support of conservative causes may have played a role in the regulatory actions of the Securities and Exchange Commission (SEC) and the IRS against him.[79]

An IRS audit of the company's 2005-2008 tax returns found an additional $23 million tax liability. In March, 2011, the Las Vegas Sands, Adelson's parent company, announced that it was the subject of an SEC and Justice Department probe for possible violations of the Foreign Corrupt Practices Act, which bars US companies from bribing foreign officials. Apparently the investigation stems from the company's employment of a Chinese official to oversee its lucrative Macau operations.[80]

Whether or not Adelson violated any law, the targeting of a major Republican donor right at the time of the election seems extremely fishy. And there are likely many other conservative donors who have been subjected to IRS retaliation. Texas Republican Senator Ted Cruz said, "I have heard from dozens of financial supporters of Gov. Romney that told me that they had never been audited in their life, and within a week, a month of it becoming public they were raising money for Mitt Romney, they discovered they were being audited." Cruz added, "Now, those are anecdotal stories, but it would be relatively simple to examine the prosecution rates of Obama donors vs. Romney donors, and, if there were sharp differentials, if it were the case that Romney donors were being audited at a much higher frequency, that would raise substantial basis to investigate further."[81]

Would these IRS audits have happened anyway? Was there a connection between Adelson's outspoken political activity and government audits? It is a hallmark of authoritarian govern-ments that they keep you guessing. One Romney donor doesn't have to guess. Frank VanderSloot, the CEO of Melaleuca Inc., a wellness-products company located in Idaho Falls, ID, gave $1 million to the Romney campaign. The Obama campaign website posted the information, accusing him — falsely — of being "a bitter foe of the gay rights movement."[82]

The Wall Street Journal reports that a week after the posting, a private investigator contacted the local Idaho courthouse seek-ing information on VanderSloot's divorces and seven lawsuits, including a civil suit against a former employee.[83]

Rush Limbaugh revealed that fifteen of Romney's top donors have been audited by the IRS, many right after their donations were disclosed. The talk show host summed it up: "We literally do have, folks, Banana Republic-type government going on here. I don't know how else to describe it. Virtually every aspect of this administration is politically oriented."[84]

WAS ROMNEY HIMSELF TARGETED?

In August of 2012, as the presidential race heated up, Senate Majority Leader Harry Reid took to the floor of the chamber to make an unusual charge against Republican presidential nom-inee, Mitt Romney. "The word's out," Reid said, "that he [Rom-ney] hasn't paid any taxes for ten years." Then he added, "let him prove that he has paid taxes, because he hasn't."[85]

At the time, Romney had not released his tax returns despite heavy pressure to do so. When they eventually were released, put-ting the lie to Reid's statement, they showed that he had paid only about 15 percent of his income in taxes, although he had donated large sums to charity, which he legally deducted. He also said that he had paid at least 13 percent in taxes for each year for the past decade.

But, in light of the release of Christine O'Donnell's tax returns and the IRS harassment of conservative groups, many have asked this question: Where did Reid get his information? Reid claimed the information came to him from someone who had once been an investor in Romney's firm, but he refused to reveal the identity of his source. And, since the statement was made on the Senate floor, it is privileged. But would Reid have been so definitive unless he has reliable information on which to base his charge?

All of this begs the question: Did the IRS seek to intervene in a presidential race on behalf of the incumbent by leaking information about his challenger? In the world of Obama, the IRS is not just a revenue collection agency — as intrusive and threatening as that can be — but it also is an instrument of political intimidation and a font of damaging information to use to destroy political opponents. Of all the abuses of this administration, the misuse of the IRS is the most dangerous.

And it's all an important part of Obama's power grab scheme to handicap the opposition and create a one-party government.

The Federal Elections Commission, the Internal Revenue Service, and the Federal Bureau of Investigation in Obama's administration have made Republican candidates and donors afraid lest their exercise of their constitutional rights lead to trouble with the law. That's an unhealthy state of affairs for a democracy. Obama is criminalizing political dissent by conservatives.

All part of the grand plan.

Point Six: Addicting the Electorate to Federal Entitlements

Like any good drug pusher, the Obama administration understands a core reality: Once somebody tries your product, the odds are that they will become hooked. And once hooked, they will structure their entire lives around getting more of what you are pushing. In the president's case, it is not heroin or cocaine that he is selling; it is an equally addictive product: federal government entitlements. Unlike previous administrations that have sought to dampen the number of Americans on entitlements in order to hold down spending, the Obama people have done they can to increase the pool of potential entitlement-addicted Americans, regardless of the impact on the deficit. There are plenty of potential new Democratic Party voters in that pool.

But they encountered a problem: Congress was not willing to appropriate any more money and refused to open the Treasury any further to entitlements (except, of course, ObamaCare). So President Obama and his cabinet have exploited every loophole they could find, weakened every administrative standard and turned a blind eye toward fraud to expand the reach of federal entitlements. Because they all realize that each time they create a new entitlement addict, they generate another vote to help their audacious power grab succeed.

According to the Congressional Research Service, spending on means-tested entitlements (which we'll call welfare) rose by 41 percent during Obama's presidency.[86] Today, the eighty-three overlapping federal welfare programs are, collectively, the largest single item in the entire federal budget, costing $750 billion, or 21 percent of Washington's spending. By contrast, Social Security costs $725 billion, Medicare comes to $480 billion, and defense spending (excluding Afghanistan) absorbs $540 billion. Counting state and local spending, welfare costs Americans $1 trillion per year.[87]

Political machines have always tried to buy electoral support, but the Obama juggernaut does it on a far more massive scale and uses taxpayer funding to do so. How, many political pundits asked, could Obama get reelected despite the economic doldrums gripping the country? Mitt Romney came closest to the truth in his famous gaffe about the spread of entitlements and their impact on the election. Speaking at a closed-door fund-raiser on May 17, 2012 — when he didn't know cameras were rolling — he said:

> There are forty-seven percent of the people who will vote for the president no matter what. All right, there are forty-seven

with him, who are dependent upon government, who believe that they are victims, who believe that government has a responsibility to care for them, who believe that they are entitled to health care, to food, to housing, to you name it. That's an entitlement. And the government should give it to them. And they will vote for this president no matter what. And I mean the president starts off with forty-eight, forty-nine and forty-eight — he starts off with a huge number. These are people who pay no income tax. Forty-seven percent of Americans pay no income tax. So our message of low taxes doesn't connect. And he'll be out there talking about tax cuts for the rich. I mean that's what they sell every four years. And so my job is not to worry about those people — I'll never convince them that they should take personal responsibility and care for their lives.[88]

These words, which might have cost Romney the election, have a lot of truth in them. But the Republican candidate, unfortunately, lumped together all those who get federal cash transfers, combining those who have earned them (e.g., Veterans benefits), contributed to them (e.g., Social Security and Medicare), and those who get them simply because they are poor (means-tested entitlements). It is, of course, only the last category that produces the kind of automatic vote Romney meant to criticize. Those who get welfare do not make up the forty-seven he charged. But they do reach to one-third of all Americans, which is still a huge number.

According to the Census Bureau, 108 million Americans (33 percent of the population) got means-tested government benefits in 2011. By contrast, only 102 million worked full-time.[89] *So the proportion of the population getting welfare from the government exceeds those getting full time paychecks!*

According to the Cato Institute, 60 percent of all Americans get more in federal money than they spend on federal taxes.[90] During Obama's first term alone, food stamp enrollment rose by 65 percent, Medicaid by 19 percent, and disability beneficiaries rose by 18 percent. During the same time, the number of employed people in the United States dropped by 0.7 percent.[91]

Here are the major federal entitlement programs:

Means Tested Government Programs, 2011[92]	
Program	**Enrollment**
Medicaid	82 million
Food Stamps	49 million
Supplementary Security Income	23 million
Women, Infants, Children	13 million
Public or subsidized housing	13 million
Welfare	6 million

Romney derived his 47 percent figure by including the 49 million who get Social Security checks, the 46 million who get Medicare benefits, the 5 million on unemployment insurance, and 3 million veterans.

But even at 33 percent, the proportion of votes effectively "bought" by the welfare state is enormous. Counting the state share of these programs, they cost almost $1 trillion.[93] The exclusively-federal share of spending on these federal programs is up 32 percent since 2008.[94] Let's keep it simple. Means-tested entitlements, or welfare, is simply taking money from a wage earning Peter to pay a usually unemployed Paul.

Much of this growth is recent, triggered by the vigorous efforts of the Obama administration to sign people up. For example, at the start of the Obama presidency, 27 million Americans got food stamps. By 2013, the number had swollen to 47 million.[95] Thirty percent have no children living with them.[96] Even when the recession theoretically ended in 2009, the number of recipients continued to rise.

The second most rapidly growing entitlement under Obama has been the Social Security Disability Insurance program. In his five years as president, so far, Obama has granted disability benefits to 5.4 million Americans.[97] His administration has pushed judges to loosen the standards and lower the bar for benefits. Each new yes creates an American with a strong stake in liberal expansion of the welfare state.

A study of the increasing rate of approvals indicates that it was the "relaxation of the medical criteria" which was the main driver of the upward rise.[98] In other words, giving benefits to people who don't deserve or need them.

Medicaid, the largest of the means-tested entitlements, had increased from 50 million enrollees in 2009 to 54 million in 2012.[99]

But that wasn't enough for the Obama White House. The president included in ObamaCare a vast expansion of the program. While states had varied widely in their coverage and eligibility standards, the law now required them to cover everyone whose income was below 133 percent of the poverty level ($15,520 for an individual and $30,590 for a family of four). Before the law passed, some states covered only up to 25 percent of the poverty level. But, in upholding the constitutionality of ObamaCare, the US Supreme Court ruled that it was unconstitutional to require states to have such high eligibility for Medicaid. The justices granted each state the right to decide on its own whether to keep its current eligibility levels or to meet the ObamaCare standard.

To induce them to increase their Medicaid caseload, the ObamaCare bill provided that the feds would pay the full cost of the new enrollees for three years and 90 percent of the next three years. After that, the states would have to pay one-third to one-half of the cost based on their economic situation.

Induced by the incentives, twenty-six states and the District of Columbia have chosen to participate in the higher standards:

Arizona, Arkansas, California, Colorado, Connecticut, Delaware, Hawaii, Illinois, Iowa, Kentucky, Maryland, Massachusetts, Michigan, Minnesota, Nevada, New Hampshire, New Jersey, New Mexico, New York, North Dakota, Ohio, Oregon, Rhode Island, Vermont, Washington, and West Virginia.

Under the new law, an estimated 3 million more Americans had signed up for Medicaid, bringing the total increase in coverage under the Obama administration to 61 million.[100] One way or another, Obama has done all he can to drive up enrollment in federal entitlement programs. The increases in food stamp, disability, and Medicaid populations are not due primarily to the economy, but to the vigorous outreach of the Obama administration. Lest there be any doubts that this increase in entitlements is related to an increase in outreach and not a growth in genuine need, evidence that the enrollments have not dropped with the recession's end should assuage them.

And, with the onset of ObamaCare, a new entitlement has been created, making millions more dependent on government largesse. By the end of the enrollment period, Washington reported that 8 million people had signed up for the program and that 80 percent of them will get subsidies from the government[101] — another 8 million people dependent on the federal government for handouts.

So here's the tally under Obama:

- 20 million more on food stamps
- 8 million more on Medicaid
- 5 million more on disability benefits
- 6 million on ObamaCare

TURNING A BLIND EYE TO FOOD STAMP FRAUD

The surge in food stamp enrollment from 27 million to almost 50 million since 2007 has also been driven by vigorous outreach efforts by the Obama administration. Eager to increase the number of Americans benefiting from entitlements, the USDA has reached out to the AmeriCorps volunteer program and has joined with numerous non-profit groups in signing people up to the program.

But, next to the explosion in beneficiaries and costs, the efforts to prevent, detect, and punish fraud are pathetic. With only forty inspectors to oversee almost 200,000 merchants that accept food stamps, the Government Accountability Office reported last summer that retailers who traffic illegally in food stamps by redeeming stamps for cash or alcohol or other prohibited items "are less likely to face criminal penalties or prosecution" than in earlier years.[102]

Beyond fraud, the administration and states have loosened eligibility requirements. You can own a car — even a Rolls — and a McMansion, and still get food stamps as long as your current income is low enough.

In thirty-five states, it doesn't matter how many assets you have or what your net worth is. Only income and family size matters. And, even in states that consider your assets in determining your eligibility, the asset ceilings are very permissive.

In Pennsylvania, for example, food stamp applicants may own one car, a house, and retirement benefits — each of any value — and not have them counted as assets for purposes of eligibility. Apart from these items, they can have up to $5,500 in assets and still qualify. Applicants are even allowed to own a second car of up to $4,650 in value. Income limits, in Pennsylvania are $14,079 for a one person household, $18,941 for two, $23,803 for three, and $28,665 for four people. Given the generous eligibility standards, there would seem to be little room left for cheating, but food stamp fraud is very widespread. James Bovard, writing in *The Wall Street Journal*, cataloged its extent:

"... Wisconsin food-stamp recipients routinely sell their benefit cards on Facebook ... and nearly 2,000 recipients claimed they lost their card six or more times in 2010 and requested replacements[103] . . . Seattle recipients were selling their cards on Craigslist or brazenly cashing them out on street corners (for 50 cents on the dollar)[104] . . . thirty percent of the inmates in the Polk County, IA, jail were collecting food stamps that were being sent to their non-jail mailing addresses in 2009.[105] . . . Two veteran employees in the New York City's Human Resources Administration were busted for concocting 1,500 fake food-stamp cases that netted them $8 million.[106] Nine Milwaukee, WI staffers plundered almost $300,000 from the program during the last five years . . ."[107]

The horror stories go on and on. Bovard charges that "the Obama administration is responding [to the wave of fraud] by cracking down [not on the fraud, but] on the state governments' anti-fraud measures. The administration is seeking to compel California, New York, and Texas to cease requiring food-stamp applicants to provide finger images."[108]

But, without a doubt, Mr. Leroy Fick is the "poster boy" for food stamps. Bovard reports, "After Mr. Fick won a $2 million lottery jackpot, the Michigan Department of Human Services ruled he could continue receiving food stamps."[109] Since he elected to take the jackpot all at once, it would not be considered income.

THE NEW EPIDEMIC: DISABILITY BENEFIT FRAUD

New Yorkers were entertained to see a photograph in *The Wall Street Journal* of former New York City police sergeant Richard Cosentino holding an enormous, newly caught swordfish as he yelled at photographers to go away. While he may have been proud of his catch, he was undoubtedly less than happy to be exposed publicly since he had claimed that he was housebound virtually, totally disabled. More than one hundred people, including seventy-two former City police officers and eight former firefighters were busted as the Manhattan District Attorney's office exposed the most massive fraud in the history of the disability program. Together these phony claims substantiated by false affidavits, cost taxpayers $400 million.[110]

The *WSJ* reports that "the plot, allegedly under way since at least 1988, involved four facilitators who helped coach hundreds of applicants on how to convince the Social Security Administration that they were entitled to monthly disability payments because they were unable to work at any job due to psychiatric conditions."[111]

Manhattan District Attorney Cyrus Vance Jr. said the defendants "coached the applicants on how to describe the symptoms of depression and anxiety during the application process. Specifically they instructed them on how to intentionally fail memory tests, how to dress when they presented themselves, and how to present their demeanor."[112] About half of the cops and firefighters involved in the scam said that their psychiatric trauma stemmed from the 9-11 Trade Center attack.

But, beyond fraud, the swelling of the ranks of those getting disability benefits is also due to changes in the law's eligibility requirements. Jimmy Carter signed the Disability Amendments Act of 1980, which encouraged tighter oversight of Social Security disability benefits. Early in Reagan's first term, the Gipper asked the Social Security Administration to step up enforcement of the new law, leading to the revocation of benefits for over one million people. There was a substantial political backlash; as a result, in 1984, Congress unanimously passed the Social Security Disability Benefits Reform Act. "It maintains our commitment to treat disabled American citizens fairly and humanely while fulfilling our obligation to the Congress and the American taxpayers to administer the disability program effectively," said Reagan upon signing the bill into law.[113]

Forbes magazine reported that because the new law placed greater importance on an applicant's own descriptions of pain and disability and allowed them to rely on their own doctors, the "overall effect was to create a giant loophole, by which an applicant's subjective claim that he was in pain, or mentally incapacitated, would be enough to claim disability."[114] Statistics show that mental health claims and those involving muscle or skeletal problems are driving the increase in disability cases. Between 1993 and 2009, the number of disability awards for cancer, circulatory diseases, or other non-mental, non-skeletal, non-muscular illnesses remained unchanged. But claims involving psychiatric or bone or muscle pain almost doubled. In fact, the number of disability awards based on these conditions now equals as many as all other complaints combined. It's not easy to fake cancer or heart disease.

There's more money in disability awards these days. The size of the disability checks being handed out has grown substantially. Now, disability claims "replace the majority of your income if you're poor and a smaller fraction of your income if you were well-paid in your previous jobs."[115] Finally, anyone on disability automatically goes on Medicare, accounting for a significant part — some estimate as much as 20 percent[116] — of the rapid run-up in Medicare spending.

Obama knows that welfare dependency breeds addiction to government handouts and leads to block voting for the Democrats. He is driving America toward the tipping point where a majority pay no taxes, are not in the labor force, and get checks from the government.

We are getting there.

PAY NO TAXES:

Romney was right that 46.4 percent of American households, representing 49.5 percent of the population, paid no federal income tax in 2011.[117] Half of those not filing taxes make less than $17,000 per year, and 80 percent earn less than $33,500. But 13 percent make between $33,500 and $59,000. Seventy-eight thousand tax filers with incomes between $211,000 and $533,000 paid no income taxes; 24,000 households with incomes of $533,000 to $2.2 million paid no income taxes, and 3,000 tax filers with incomes above $2.2 million paid no income taxes.[118]

Not that these folks escape taxes entirely. Most pay FICA and Medicare taxes. Only 18 percent of American households escape any income or payroll taxes entirely.[119]

NOT IN THE LABOR FORCE:

Today, 37.2 percent of the adult population is not in the labor force at all. They are unemployed and not looking for work. Since Obama's presidency began, the proportion of Americans out of the labor market has increased from 33.7 to its current level. Put another way, about 9 million Americans have dropped out of the labor force since Obama took office.[120] Most of these are people who have just given up on the possibility of finding work.

We are becoming a nation of non-workers.

GETTING GOVERNMENT BENEFITS:

While 46 percent of Americans get some form of government benefits, 33 percent get means-tested benefits — i.e., welfare.

So, to sum up, 49.5 percent pay no income taxes. Forty-six get government checks. Thirty-three percent get welfare. And thirty-seven percent don't work and don't want to work. Under Obama, 10 million more people get welfare and 9 million fewer are in the labor force.

We're beginning to look like a European country already!

Point Seven: Changing the Rules of the Senate to Create a Compliant Judiciary

One of the obstacles to Obama's plan for one-party government is the refusal of many federal courts to rubber-stamp his unconstitutional policies. In order to overcome that, he has nominated extremely liberal candidates for federal judgeships. Many of these have been rejected by the Senate.

Presidents have always had the power to appoint judges, but the Senate has vigorously used its own constitutional authority to refuse to confirm many of these nominations. Since our Constitution took effect, the Senate has refused to confirm about one-quarter of the Supreme Court nominations submitted by the president.[121] Because the president also nominates men and women to fill the 600 District Court judgeships and the 200 Appellate Court positions, rejections at those levels are even more numerous.

When the Constitution was written, no one anticipated the rise of political parties and it seemed reasonable to require a majority vote in the Senate to confirm judicial appointments. But with the rise of parties, a danger emerged that one party might control both the presidency and the Senate and rubber-stamp judicial appointments without the scrutiny our system of checks and balances demands. What was to stop the president and the Senate — if controlled by the same party — from usurping power, undermining the Constitution, and then appointing and confirming judges who would let their measures stand, approving unconstitutional executive actions just because their party demanded it?

The only thing preventing a runaway judiciary was the rule in the US Senate allowing unlimited debate. The filibuster, once reserved for Southern objections to civil rights measures, emerged as a key check and balance on unbridled executive power, all the more essential when the same party ran the Senate and the White House.

Under the Senate rules, a vote of closure is required to shut off debate and force a vote on a judicial confirmation (or any other piece of legislation). Once closure required a two-thirds vote of the upper chamber, but over the years, it was modified so sixty votes is enough.

But being checked and balanced — sharing power in our democracy — is not what President Obama or Senate Majority

Leader Harry Reid has in mind. Especially after the Democrats lost control of the House of Representatives in 2010, their bid to transform America into a one-party state required a rapid expansion of executive power, coupled with a compliant judiciary ready to approve the usurpation.

The filibuster stood in the way, empowering the forty-five senators in the Republican minority to block judicial confirmations as long as they stuck together. So despite having a comfortable majority in the Senate, Obama found that he couldn't push through his more controversial and partisan nominees for the judiciary. Notwithstanding the Democratic Party control of the Senate during his entire presidency, Obama has only been able to get 76 percent of his nominations to the bench confirmed. By comparison, President Bush-43 (whose party controlled the Senate for six of his eight years in office) won confirmation of 92 percent of his judicial nominations, and President Clinton (who only had control for two of eight years) prevailed 81 percent of the time.[122] As Obama's more controversial nominees sat waiting for confirmation, the number of judicial vacancies piled up. Of 874 judgeships in the country, 95 were vacant at the start of 2014.[123]

The nation's second most important court is the DC Circuit Court where challenges to federal regulatory decisions are heard. With Obama allocating to himself and his appointees unprecedented powers to issue executive orders, this court acquires pivotal importance. By the end of 2012, when the key cases started to appear, eight of the eleven judgeships on the court had been filled — four by Democrats and four by Republicans. With an even partisan division, it looked like the president's regulations and executive orders might get an impartial hearing. But impartiality wasn't good enough for Obama or Reid. They tried to jam through three highly partisan democratic liberals for the vacancies on the DC Circuit Court. Republicans resisted and denied the three the sixty votes necessary. Since the Court's workload was way down, the Republicans even suggested reducing the number of judges to eight, leaving the balance in place.

But Obama and Reid had other plans. On November 20, 2013, Senate Democrats voted to block filibusters to judicial nominations. By a vote of 52–48 (with every Republican voting no) the Senate changed its two hundred-year-old rule permitting unlimited debate for judicial nominations below the Supreme Court level. (Should there be a Supreme Court vacancy while Obama controls the Senate, you can bet that the filibuster will be banned there also.)

Senate Republican leader Mitch McConnell (R-KY) spoke for the outraged Senate Republicans calling the move a "power grab" and a "sad day in the history of the Senate."[124] Senator Lamar Alexander (R-TN) said it best: "It's another raw exercise of political power to permit the majority to do anything it wants whenever it wants to do it."[125] A few months before banning filibusters for judicial nominations, Reid and the Democrats jammed through a rule change that also barred them in battles over presidential appointments to executive branch agencies. But, lurking in the background is the more dire of threats: An end to filibusters of Supreme Court nominations and banning them in the passage of simple legislation. Obama and Reid will brook no opposition. No rule, precedent, tradition, or even fundamental precept of our democracy is to be allowed to stand on the path of their march toward one-party rule.

Point Eight: Intimidating the Media

Although no president has routinely attained the level of favorable coverage that Obama has had, the media still falls somewhat short of outright adulation. But, thin skinned to criticism of any kind, Obama wants nothing short of total media approval. Fawning isn't enough. The president wants absolute adoration.

He recognizes that key to his goal of a one-party government is also a one-party media. And he is determined to control the "free" press until he gets it. To perpetuate his partisan control of government, Obama moved aggressively as the 2012 election intimidates the news media to make it toe the line.

But, beyond intimidation, Obama has a more insidious goal: To control the media's sources, particularly those in his own government. Presidents have always torn their hair out — when they had some — over unauthorized leaks by their own staff.

President Reagan famously said that the ship of state was the only one that leaked from the top. But Obama has taken the war against leaks to a new level by criminalizing them and by secretly seizing the phone records of media outlets to track down their sources and punish them.

Why should we be so concerned about protecting the rights of leakers? Because unless we get information from committed citizens who want the world to hear the truth, we have only the official word of the administration to rely upon. And the "official word" is almost always colored by the political message of the White House. If our media is to do more than just transmit administration press releases, it needs the ability to use anonymous leakers who want to tell the truth.

OBAMA'S WAR ON THE ASSOCIATED PRESS

The most blatant — and widely reported — example of the heavy hand of executive power was the seizure of the phone records of the Associated Press for April and May of 2012. As the election campaign heated up, the Justice Department secretly seized the phone records of reporters and editors of the Associated Press, the entity through which most newspapers in America get their news.

The subpoenas were not only aimed at intimidating the reporters and their bosses, but were also aimed at putting fear into the hearts of those executive branch employees who would leak information to the media.

The off-the-record flow of information from administration officials has bedeviled presidents for decades. But Obama has broken new ground by prosecuting six executive branch employees for leaking — more than all previous administrations combined.

But the AP seizures are unprecedented. By examining the records the Justice Department seized, Obama's people were able to tell exactly who was leaking to whom and, by inference, about what. The real harm, however, is that government officials now know that their secret conversations with the media could become the subject of administration scrutiny and prosecution should they happen to fall into one of these record seizure dragnets in the future. Gary B. Pruitt, the CEO of the Associated Press, described the chilling effect of the seizure on journalism. Pruitt said that the government is sending a message to officials "that if you talk to the press, we're going to go after you . . . officials who would normally talk to us, and people we would talk to in the normal course of news gathering, are already saying to us that they're a little reluctant to talk to us; they fear that they will be monitored by the government."[126] Pruitt feared that this censorship directly contradicted the intent of the First Amendment and would lead to "limited and biased information."[127] Well, that's exactly what President Obama and Attorney General Eric Holder had in mind. Writing to Holder to protest, Pruitt said:

> There can be no possible justification for such an overbroad collection of the telephone communications of the Associated Press and its reporters. These records potentially reveal communications with confidential sources across all of the news-gathering activities undertaken by the AP during a two-month period, provide a road map to AP's news-gathering operations, and disclose information about AP's activities and operations that the government has no conceivable right to know.[128]

The Justice Department subpoenas were issued in secret and it was not until a year later that the AP learned about them, giving the news agency no opportunity to contest them or to seek a judicial determination of their constitutionality.

The Justice Department's justification for the subpoenas was transparently flimsy. The AP story that triggered the subpoenas was published on May 7, 2012. It reported that the administration had foiled an al Qaeda plot to blow up a bomb on an airplane bound for the United States. The story reported that "intelligence services detected the scheme as it took shape in mid-April, officials said, and the explosive device was seized in the Middle East outside Yemen about a week ago before it could be deployed."[129]

Why was the administration so angry about the AP story? Not because of any national security concerns or any desire to protect its operations from public view, but their fury was triggered because Obama himself wanted to announce the operation and the AP story jumped the gun. The AP broke the story on a Monday afternoon. The news organization "said that it had uncovered the existence of the bomb last week, but that the White House and the CIA had asked it not to publish the news immediately because the intelligence operation was still under way. Once officials said those concerns had been allayed, the AP reported, it decided to disclose the plot despite requests from the Obama administration to wait for an official announcement on Tuesday."[130]

All the AP had done was to deny Obama bragging rights and a victory lap. And, to punish them for their actions, its phone records were seized for two months!

Obama was not just trying to muzzle the AP. He was also trying to intimidate anyone who leaked to AP in these crucial pre-election months. All over Washington, anonymous sources in the government were searching their memories to see of their phone calls with AP reporters were among the records seized. The message was clear: If you leak, we can find out. You are taking your career in your hands and risking it all. So think twice before you pick up the phone and tell a reporter what is really going on in the people's government.

OBAMA'S WAR ON FOX NEWS

President Obama has frequently denounced the FOX News Channel, but in 2013, he used the Justice Department to go after FOX News reporter James Rosen. Rosen had received information from State Department contractor Stephen Kim about an internal State Department document predicting that North Korea would conduct a nuclear test in response to the toughening of sanctions against it by the West. The administration contended that Rosen's story revealed that we had a source in North Korea that permitted us to obtain the information despite Pyongyang's penchant for tight secrecy. Rosen did not indicate whether his story was based on electronic or human intelligence, but the feds were outraged nonetheless. The Justice Department got a search warrant to probe Rosen and identify his source. The feds insisted on keeping the warrant secret even after two federal judges ordered them to tell the reporter. Eventually, a third judge agreed to the secrecy, but the story came out anyway.

The feds prosecuted Kim and even mulled bringing charges against Rosen. The message again: Be careful who you talk to in Obama's Washington.

The Rosen case was only the most grievous manifestation of Obama's ongoing war against FOX News. Attacking a news organization more vociferously and specifically than any president has ever done, the president repeatedly seeks to discredit and intimidate his critics at FOX News and elsewhere.

- On October 15, 2008, as his election loomed, Obama told *The New York Times* that "I am convinced that if there were no FOX News, I might be two or three points higher in the polls. If I were watching FOX News, I wouldn't vote for me, right? Because the way I'm portrayed 24/7 is as a freak! I am the latte-sipping, *New York Times*-reading, Volvo-driving, no-gun-owning, effete, politically correct, arrogant liberal. Who wants somebody like that?"[131]

- In an interview with *Rolling Stone* magazine right before the 2012 elections, Obama said that FOX News was "ultimately destructive for the long-term growth of a country that has a vibrant middle class and is competitive in the world."[132]

- Just as ObamaCare was set for its disastrous, October 1, 2013, launch, Obama blamed its increasingly negative image on FOX News: "If you talk to somebody who said, 'Well, I don't know — I was watching FOX News and they said this was horrible. I promise you: If you go on the website . . . even if you didn't vote for me, I'll bet you'll sign up for that health care plan."[133]

- On January 27, 2013, Obama said that FOX News and radio host Rush Limbaugh were obstructing bipartisan cooperation in Washington. He said, "If a Republican member of Congress is not punished on FOX News or by Rush Limbaugh for working with a Democrat on a bill of common interest, then you'll see more of them doing it."[134]

- On October 23, 2013, democratic operative Bob Beckel, who co-hosts The Five show on FOX News, said he was "absolutely bludgeoned" in a phone call with an administration staffer for criticizing Obama for not delaying the rollout of his health care program until it could proceed more smoothly.[135]

- On January 23, 2014, Obama said "I'm not the caricature that you see on FOX News or Rush Limbaugh."[136]

- On Super Bowl Sunday, February 2, 2014, FOX News' Bill O'Reilly interviewed the president and asked about the IRS' targeting of conservative groups. The president answered,

"These kind of things keep resurfacing in part because you and your TV station will promote them."[137]

Presidents have often complained about their treatment by the media. Some, like Nixon singled out one organ — in his case *The Washington Post* — for special scorn. But none have given such public and repeated voice to these attacks on a specific organ of the national news media.

Why is Obama attacking FOX News with such frequency? Obviously, intimidation is part of his goal. By his loud attacks, he hopes to make FOX News second guess its critical attitude toward him and his policies.

But part of his goal is to stop people from watching FOX News by repeatedly characterizing it as an extremist station filled with twenty-four hour propaganda.

He's right to fear FOX News. Far from just preaching to the choir of conservatives, survey research shows that its reach is far broader over the entire spectrum of public opinion. While 75 percent of Republicans say they watch the station either "every day" or "several times each week," so do 50 percent of Independents and, most surprisingly, 25 percent of self-described Democrats.[138] By affixing a warning label to the network, Obama hopes to lower its viewership and concentrate it among conservatives. It's not working. FOX News has consistently outperformed the other cable news networks. For example, the Nielsen ratings for January 23, 2014, revealed that 2.4 million people watched FOX News during prime time, compared to only 1.0 million who watched MSNBC and a mere 490,000 who tuned to CNN.[139]

Despite Obama's constant denunciation of FOX News, it is the single most trusted television network in the nation. A survey by a democratic-leaning group, Public Policy Polling (PPP), found that 35 percent of Americans identified FOX News as the television network they trust more than any other. PBS came in second at 14 percent, ABC at 11 percent, CNN at 10 percent, CBS at 9 percent, MSNBC at 6 percent and NBC at 3 percent. Comedy Central was at 6 percent, making it twice as trusted as the NBC television network.[140]

OBAMA CENSORS NEWS PHOTOGRAPHERS

That which he doesn't attack, Obama seeks to censor. Despite pledging to have the "most transparent administration in history,"[141] Obama has sharply limited the rights of news photographers to take his picture. Instead, the administration will only permit official White House photographers to take the president or first lady's picture. Ron Fornier, of the *National Journal*, describes the difference. "Unlike media photographers, official White House photographers are paid by taxpayers and report to the president. Their job is to make Obama look good. They are propagandists — in the purest sense of the word."[142] Indeed, *The New York Times* photographer Doug Mills reportedly complained about the restrictions to Jay Carney, Obama's press secretary. Upon hearing Carney defend the limitations, he said "you guys are just like Tass,"[143] referring to the old Kremlin news agency under communism. Fournier writes that "Obama's image-makers are . . . subverting independent news organizations that hold the president accountable."[144]

The New York Times and the White House Correspondent's Association wrote in protest: "As surely as if they were placing a hand over a journalist's camera lens, officials in this administration are blocking the public from having an independent view of important functions of the executive branch of government." *The Times* warned that the restrictions "raise constitutional concerns" and amount to "arbitrary restraint and unwarranted interference on legitimate newsgathering activities."[145]

The sheer vanity of trying to control pictures of the president is unbecoming to a republic. But the precedent of permitting news organizations to cover only what the White House wants is chilling. Whether it is seizing phone lines of media outlets to determine who are their sources or banning media photographers, Obama displays a third world despot's desire to control the news.

THE FCC TRIES TO INTIMIDATE THE NEWS INDUSTRY

The most overt — and threatening — of Obama's attempts to structure media coverage came in February of 2014 when the Federal Communications Commission (FCC) proposed monitoring the nation's radio, television, and print media newsrooms to be sure that they were devoting adequate coverage to the type of news the FCC wanted to be reported.

For over two hundred years, Americans have always been confident that their news was not being filtered by government censors. But the Obama administration proposed to change all that. The FCC actually tried to use its jurisdiction over radio and television broadcasting to require them to shape the content of the news to its liking under the questionable theory that they use airwaves that belong to the public. And the FCC actually claimed the authority to regulate newspapers, a novel and unconstitutional violation of the First Amendment. This was an extraordinary step to take, even for the Obama administration.

After a national outcry and uproar, the agency backed down from its plans to survey all news media to determine if the news coverage met with their approval . . . But the FCC remains determined to expand its regulatory reach over the media.

In years past, under the so-called "Fairness Doctrine," the agency tried to interfere with news coverage by demanding that it fit its definition of "balanced" between opposite points of view. Ever since the Fairness Doctrine was eliminated in 1987, the left has cast about for a way to let the FCC regulate the content of public information over the air waves, in particular, by controlling talk radio, the bastion of conservatism on the air.

In February 2014, it looked as if it may have created the ideal vehicle. FCC Commissioner Ajit Pai, who opposed the idea, explained what they were up to:

"... FCC [has] proposed an initiative to thrust the federal government into news-rooms across the country. With its 'Multi-Market Study of Critical Information Needs,' or CIN, the agency plans to send researchers to grill reporters, editors, and station owners about how they decide which stories to run."[146]

The purpose of CIN is to determine "the process by which stories are selected" and how often stations cover "critical information needs," along with "perceived station bias" and "perceived responsiveness to underserved populations."[147]

The FCC planned to ask station managers, news directors, journalists, anchors, and others (on-air and behind-the-scenes) dozens of intrusive questions about their "news philosophy;" "who decides which stories are covered; how much influence reporters and anchors have in deciding which stories to cover; how much community input influences news coverage decisions; etc.[148]

Based on these questions, the FCC proposed to give stations guidance on how to shape their news coverage.

While the suggestions would have been voluntary, as Commissioner Pai points out, the demands of the FCC are hard to ignore since "they would be out of business without an FCC license, which must be renewed every eight years."[149]

Even assuming that the FCC is right to police radio and television news, it has no right to snoop on newspapers since they are protected by the First Amendment and involve no use of public airwaves.

For now, an alert public has beaten back the FCC power grab effort to impose censorship, but more attacks on the First Amendment are undoubtedly coming.

A critical press is an impediment to one-party government and must be controlled.

Point Nine: Rigging the Rules to Give Labor Unions More Power and More Members

Organized labor, always a sure ally of the Democrats, has been in full retreat in recent years. They're basically going out of business. The numbers are stunning: The proportion of private sector workers who belong to labor unions has dropped from 35 percent in 1945 to less than 7 percent today.[150] That's an 80 percent decrease in union members in non-government jobs.

Public employees have picked up some of the slack. More than 40 percent of state and local public employees are unionized and, today, there are more public employees than private sector workers in unions. But even that sector has run into serious problems in places like Wisconsin, where legislation passed by Governor Scott Walker limited the collective bargaining rights of government employees and prohibited the mandatory collection of union dues. So labor unions are frantically trying to do anything possible to sign up new members.

And President Obama is right there with them. One of his central goals has always been to support and encourage the expansion of the number of workers in unions. He does this for two reasons: (1) to subject them to the political discipline of unions and their support of the Democratic Party, and, (2) to add their dues to the union's powerful political action committees' coffers that contribute millions to the Democratic Party.

This fits in perfectly with his overall goal of one-party government. Ever since the passage of the National Labor Relations Act of 1935, enacted during FDR's New Deal, the National Labor Relations Board (NLRB) has been the governing body that adjudicated disputes between labor and management and other aspects of industrial relations. Sometimes veering toward labor and, at other times, tilting toward management, the NLRB has umpired disputes well since its inception.

But Obama has tried to change the NLRB into a cudgel to force workers to join unions, often over their objections. His first attempt was to change the law to tilt much more toward unions. As a senator, Obama was a sponsor of the Employee Free Choice Act and promoted it as President. That bill would have eliminated the secret ballot in union elections. After Obama's 2008 election, this bill was the labor movement's biggest legislative priority. But when that bill failed, even in his sixty vote, Democratic Senate, Obama resorted, as usual, to executive action. (Only fifty-nine senators voted for the bill.) For decades, when a union tried to organize a plant, it worked to get employees to sign cards or petitions asking for an election to determine if the workforce wanted a union shop. If more than 30 percent signed, management was required to hold a secret ballot election. Now the unions wanted to add a rule eliminating the secret ballot election entirely, if more than 50 percent of the workers signed cards endorsing unionization.

Why a vote when a majority have already signed? Because history shows that what workers say when they are confronted by their co-workers or foremen with a pen and a card, their response is often quite different from what they do in a closed, secret ballot. In 2009, when the legislation was pending, unions won 64 percent of the secret ballot elections,[151] but, in more than one third of the cases, the opponents of the union prevailed — even though they had just signed up to force an election. Indeed, just recently in February 2014, the workers at the VW plant in Chattanooga, TN, voted to reject representation by the United Auto Workers by 626 voting yes and 712 voting no.[152] But, a majority had earlier signed cards seeking an election. So their rejection affirmed the importance of the secret ballot. Big labor still desperately wants to dispense with the secret ballot and let the cards suffice to show worker interest in organizing.

So, once more, Obama plotted a power grab and set about to act without Congress. The NLRB consists of four members that by law must be half Republican and half Democrat, with a fifth member, the chairman, appointed by the president. The two

Republican, holdovers from the Bush administration, were opposed to Obama's card check proposal, but Obama was confident that he could still control the board with his democratic majority.

It didn't work out that way.

As soon as Obama made clear his intention to use the NLRB to jam through his proposals that had just been rejected by Congress, Senate Republicans dug in their heels and refused to confirm his nominees to the Board (two democratic members and the democratic chairman). With only two members sitting, the Board lacked a quorum and could not legally take any action. But legalities proved no problem for Obama as he used his recess appointment power to name three new members to the board, all liberal Democrats.

OBAMA'S "RECESS" APPOINTMENTS

The Constitution authorizes the president to make recess appointments when the Senate is not in session. The provision stems from the time of our Founding Fathers, when calling the Senate into session was a laborious affair, which required members to travel long distances over bumpy roads. Because of this difficulty, the president was permitted to make temporary appointments when the Senate was out of session and, therefore, not available.

In this case, the "recess" in question was not really a recess at all. In fact, at the time in January 2012, the Senate was deliberately holding a *pro forma* session every few days precisely to prevent Obama from claiming the Senate was in recess. The appointments were challenged in three federal appeals courts and each found that Obama had "overstepped his bounds."[153] One of the issues was who decides, for purposes of a recess appointment, whether the Senate is in recess — the president or the Senate. Even Obama's liberal Supreme Court appointee, Elena Kagan "suggested that it is the Senate's role to determine whether they're in recess."[154] At this writing, the case is on appeal to the Supreme Court and the oral argument certainly gave opponents of the president's high-handed action some grounds for optimism.

For once, Obama's power grab just might not work.

Ultimately, the president and Senate Majority Leader Harry Reid despaired of ever being able to confirm Obama's appointees to the NLRB and the Senate Democratic majority eliminated the right to filibuster presidential appointees. So Obama's radicals were confirmed. (But regulations adopted by the recess appointees are in limbo pending the Court ruling on the legality of their appointments. A ruling against Obama could result in the invalidation of hundreds of decisions made by the Obama appointees).

But, meanwhile, the newly constituted NLRB is doing all it can to help boost union chances in organizing elections.

THE NLRB "AMBUSH RULE"

In particular, it is pushing the "ambush" rule, which requires elections on unionization to be held just twenty-one days after a petition of an election is filed. The provision gives the union all the time it needs to prepare for a union election, since it controls the timing of the petition filing. Employers, who now have forty-two days to campaign against the unionization, would have only half the time.

Republican Congressmen John Kline (R-MN) and Phil Roe (R-TN), the chairmen of the relevant House committees, denounced the proposed rule saying that "this ambush election scheme will make it virtually impossible for workers to make an informed decision in union elections," and that "this flawed proposal will stifle employer free speech and worker free choice, and that the only entity that stands to gain is Big Labor."[155]

But the forces opposing the spread of unionization, particularly among public employees, have been vigorously fighting back.

In Wisconsin, Governor Scott Walker (R) led a successful effort to end state collection of union dues for public employees, leaving it up to the workers to decide if they want to pay the union or not. Walker's reforms limited collective bargaining between public unions and Wisconsin state and local governments and school districts solely to issues about wages, barring unions from bargaining over pensions, health coverage, hours, sick leave, or vacations.

The results of the labor changes have been electrifying. School districts and counties have saved $2 billion[156] and school districts can finally fire ineffective teachers and adopt pay-for-performance policies. As a result, there have been fewer layoffs of police or teachers.

The new law also requires public employee unions (police and fire are exempted) to get re-certified to represent their workers on a regular basis. Of the 400 unions and locals that have held re-certification elections up through December of 2013, the union has lost in 80 percent of the cases.[157]

Overall, union membership has dropped by more than half. For example, Local 1 of AFSME (American Federation of State, County, and Municipal Employees), located in Madison Wisconsin, has seen its membership drop from 1,000 to a mere 122.[158]

On the national level, home care workers have brought a suit that has been heard by the Supreme Court against laws that require public employees to pay dues to a union whether they want to or not. The workers say the law violates their freedom of association.

THE UAW DEFEAT AT THE VOLKSWAGEN PLANT IN CHATTANOOGA

Meanwhile, on the industrial union front, labor has been running into big obstacles as it seeks to expand, especially in the South. The refusal of the workers at the Chattanooga, TN VW plant to embrace the UAW is a case in point.

The situation there was highly unusual. This wasn't a case where the employer vigorously fought the union. To the contrary, at VW, the plant management had actually endorsed unionization, echoing the international policies of its German owners that encouraged worker's councils where unions participated in running factories.

But the workers weren't buying it. Many cited the UAW's role in the demise of the Detroit auto industry by insisting on wage and benefit levels that left their companies uncompetitive internationally.

Mike Jarvis, a plant worker, said the opposition to the union arose spontaneously: "It just spread. I told two people who told four people who told eight people, like a pyramid kind of thing."[159]

Immediately after the defeat, the UAW appealed to the NLRB, claiming that there was a concerted effort by outside groups and one of the Senators from Tennessee to influence the election. The union claimed that the election had, therefore, been unfair.

But in a move that surprised everyone, the UAW withdrew its appeal on the day the NLRB hearing on the appeal for a new election was to begin.

Sometimes, power grabs don't work at all.

NLRB WANTS TO CONTROL NON-UNION WORKPLACES, TOO

Lately, the NLRB is scheming to expand its jurisdiction over non-union workplaces by opposing employer policies that could be interpreted as chilling employee rights under Section 7 of the Labor Relations Act, which protects "employee's right to engage in 'concerted activities' for the purpose of 'mutual aid or protection.'"[160] Reading the statue with typical Obama overreach, the Board is trying to inject itself into non-union work places by reviewing employee handbooks. The labor police are particularly focusing on employer rules such as:

- "Confidentiality policies that prohibit employees from discussing their wages and/or disciplinary action taken by the company"

- Policies prohibiting 'gossiping' by employees"

- Complaint policies requiring employees follow internal grievance procedures"

- Policies prohibiting 'fraternization' by employees"

- Dress codes prohibiting union insignia from being worn"

- Policies restricting employees' use of social media (a particularly hot topic for today's employers for several reasons)"

- At-will employment policies that can be construed as not allowing an employee to change his or her 'at-will' status through collective bargaining"

- Nondisparagement policies prohibiting employees from 'disparaging' their employer"

- Policies prohibiting 'inappropriate' postings online or on company intranets"

- Bullying policies that can be applied broadly to prohibit speech"

- Policies prohibiting solicitation and distribution during time outside of work or off company premises"

- Broadly worded policies requiring 'respectful' and 'appropriate' conduct."[161]

So far, Obama's attempts to expand the reach of labor unions so as to bolster the Democratic Party vote and financial base have largely failed due to strong Republican opposition in the Senate and an increasingly skeptical Supreme Court. But one thing is certain: He will keep trying.

Point Ten: Eliminate the Electoral College

A quiet scheme to boldly grab power — blandly called the National Popular Vote Movement — has been gradually gaining force outside of public view. The Popular Vote Movement is determined to change the way we elect presidents. Its main purpose is to maximize the power of big city, democratic machines, which would also maximize voter fraud. This power grab would fundamentally change our Constitution without having to formally amend it.

We elect our presidents now, not through the popular vote, but using the Electoral College. Each state is assigned a number of electors equal to the number of its Senators and Congressmen combined. (The District of Columbia, having no congressional representation, gets three electoral votes).

The electors may vote as they choose, although most states require them to vote for the candidate who carried their state. Only four times in our history has a candidate won the popular vote but lost the Electoral College (1824, 1876, 1888, and 2000).

But now Democrats are asking state legislatures to pass legislation requiring their state's electors to vote for the winner of the national popular vote, irrespective of who carried their own particular state. These laws will take effect and become binding on the electors when states whose electoral strength represents a majority of the Electoral College — 270 votes — have passed similar laws.

Once that happens, the Electoral College will remain in the Constitution, but as an anachronistic appendix — a mere formality. With a majority of the electors committed to voting for the winner of the national popular vote, the Electoral College won't matter.

This is a flagrant end run around the cumbersome requirements to pass a constitutional amendment. The formal procedure for amending the US Constitution requires the assent of two-thirds of the House and the Senate and the concurrence of three-quarters of the states (as expressed by the majority vote of their legislatures). But the National Popular Vote Movement seeks to bypass that procedure. Congress would not even be consulted and only enough states to constitute a majority of the

Electoral College — not three-quarters — would be needed to pass the change. This backdoor approach to amending the Constitution has never happened before in our history, but Obama's plans to grab power know no limits.

So far, ten states with 161 electoral votes have passed this bill — New York, Hawaii, Illinois, Maryland, Massachusetts, New Jersey, Washington state, Vermont, California, and Rhode Island. The District of Columbia has also agreed. Legislation has passed only one house in a number of other states. While most of the support has come from Democrats, some Republicans have been fooled into supporting the measure. The Republican-controlled state Senate in New York, for example, passed the measure in 2014.

How would the legislation give the Democratic Party an advantage?

Under the current system, the focus of any presidential campaign usually quickly boils down to a handful of swing states — Florida, Ohio, New Mexico, Colorado, Nevada, Iowa, Indiana, North Carolina, New Hampshire, and Pennsylvania — where history has shown that either party has a chance at victory. As a result, presidential candidates tend to ignore even populous states whose vote is a preordained conclusion. Democrats know they will carry New York, Illinois and California and Republicans are equally certain they will prevail in Texas, so there's no point in extensively campaigning there.

And, the really large, powerhouse, democratic, urban political machines — Chicago, New York, San Francisco, Baltimore, Detroit, and the other large California cities — rarely get much funding or attention from national campaigns. Of course, the Republicans, too, carry their share of cities, but most of their strength is concentrated in more rural areas.

Look at a color coded map of political preferences in America. You see vast swatches of red (Republican) and only a few dabs of blue (Democrat). The democratic vote is highly concentrated in a number of large urban areas. But were we to choose our presidents by popular vote, these urban centers would be much more important and Democrats would work hard to bring out the maximum possible vote. Turnout in inner cities would soar and Republicans would be at a great disadvantage. And the opportunities for fraud would multiply. If the entire election ever came down to a single state or a mere handful (as happened in 2000), scrutiny would fall heavily on the votes in each corner of the swing state. Voter fraud will be hard to conceal since every ballot box in the state will be under a magnifying glass.

But if the national popular vote is to be the deciding factor, voter fraud would be much harder to catch, spread, as it would be, over the entire nation. Every urban machine in every state would struggle to maximize its vote, sometimes by fair means and sometimes not.

Recognizing this reality, the Republican National Committee voted unanimously to recommend to state legislators that they oppose the National Popular Vote Bill when it comes up in their jurisdiction. But Obama's people will continue to push it. Should the Democratic Party ever win heavily at the state legislative level, look for it to emasculate the Electoral College.

It's yet one more big power grab.

And, if all else fails, Obama's ace in the hole might be his ability to declare marshall law . . .

Without a doubt, this is the scariest of the Obama power grabs — his assumption of broad martial law powers. Writing in *The Washington Times*, columnist Jeffrey T. Kuhner warns of the impact of executive order 13603, signed by President Obama on March 16, 2012.

"President Obama has given himself the powers to declare martial law — especially in the event of a war with Iran. It is a sweeping power grab that should worry every American."[162]

The order, entitled the National Defense Resources Preparedness Order, is "stunning in its audacity and a flagrant violation of the Constitution."[163]

Kuhner reports that it provides that in national emergency situations the "federal government has the authority to take over almost every aspect of American society. Food, livestock, farming equipment, manufacturing, industry, energy, transportation, hospitals, health care facilities, water resources, defense and construction — all of it could fall under the full control of Mr. Obama. The order empowers the president to dispense these vast resources as he sees fit during a national crisis."[164]

The order's preamble states that "the United States must have an industrial and technological base capable of meeting national defense requirements and capable of contributing to the technological superiority of its national defense equipment in peacetime and in times of national emergency. The domestic industrial and technological base is the foundation for national defense preparedness. The authorities provided in the act shall be used to strengthen this base and to ensure it is capable of responding to the national defense needs of the United States."[165] Kuhner warns that with the possibility of war with Iran, the chances that Obama could use the order are quite real.

Under the terms of the order, Jim Garrison, writing in *The Huffington Post* explains that:

- The Secretary of Defense has power over all water resources.

- The Secretary of Commerce has power over all material services and facilities, including construction materials.

- The Secretary of Transportation has power over all forms of civilian transportation.

- The Secretary of Agriculture has power over food resources and facilities, livestock plant health resources, and the domestic distribution of farm equipment.

- The Secretary of Health and Human Services has power over all health resources.

- The Secretary of Energy has power over all forms of energy.[166]

The executive order even stipulates that in the event of conflict between the secretaries in using these powers, the president will determine the resolution through his national security team.

Could there be any greater power grab?

Obama's supporters argue that the new executive order simply updates a very similar one signed by President Clinton in 1993 (order 12909). They say that the only real change is in the designation of which cabinet members are to be responsible for which sectors of the economy and the military in the event of a national emergency. They say that there are now new departments that didn't exist back then (like Homeland Security) and that the order needed to be updated. Presidential Press Secretary Jay Carney called the order "a fairly standard and routine piece of business."[167]

So why the fuss? Given the president's abuse of his other powers, his use of the machinery of government to intimidate his opponents, and his willingness to stretch whatever powers he has to the Constitutional breaking point, the executive order assumes a new perspective.

For all of his expansion of presidential power in the Patriot Act, there is no evidence that George W. Bush ever abused his office to implement a partisan agenda. Not even his worst enemy would accuse Bill Clinton of coveting greater power as president.

But Obama's record — especially in the days since the order was issued two years ago — give us all reason to pause when we realize how much power we are allowing this president to seize. The potential power grab here is enormous and becomes virtually unstoppable once it starts. It makes his other power grabs seem downright amateurish.

TOWARD ONE-PARTY GOVERNMENT

Taken together, the Obama administration's ten-part strategy is moving America ever closer to his goal of one-party government:

- If the president can decide which laws he wants to enforce and on whom he wishes to enforce them . . .

- If the president can make laws on his own, without even asking Congress . . .

- If ethnic minorities attuned to Obama's agenda cast an ever-larger share of the vote, many of them having entered the country illegally . . .

- If the integrity of the ballot box is compromised by widespread voter fraud and those in power turn a blind eye . . .

- If opposition groups are harassed and audited by the IRS and driven into silence . . .

- If an ever-larger proportion of Americans are dependent on the government handouts that Obama offers and Republicans largely oppose . . .

- If the United States Senate is fundamentally changed from a place where opposition views are heard to one in which they are ignored, and if the body is stripped of its ability to scrutinize federal judicial appointments . . .

- If the media is blocked, intimidated, and denigrated and its ability to criticize the government wanes . . .

- If the government rigs the rules so more Americans are forced to join labor unions . . .

- If the president can, unilaterally, declare a state of emergency and give himself martial law authority to govern then we are coming ever closer to one-party government and the tyranny it always brings with it

PART II

Obama's Regulatory Power Grab

M UCH OF OBAMA'S POWER GRAB is taking place out of sight of elected institutions in the depths of the federal executive branch agencies through new regulations.

Taxes dominate our political dialogue. Conservatives press Congressmen and Senators to sign pledges not to raise them. President Obama relentlessly pushes for more taxes, while the Republican House just as forcefully pushes back. But while all this controversy swirls over taxation, the equally important field of federal government regulation gets relatively little publicity and generates less controversy.

Yet, while Washington collects $3 trillion in taxes each year,[1] the regulations it imposes cost another $1.9 trillion.[2]

Taxes, of course, need to be voted on by an elected House and an elected Senate and signed by an elected president. But regulations pass into force without ever being touched by an elected official.

Nominally, they are approved by an unelected cabinet secretary or an agency head appointed by the president, but, in fact, they rarely rise to the level of even his or her approval. Most regulations are fashioned in the bowels of the executive branch agencies, usually by lifetime civil servants who, after years working for a particular agency, often have tunnel vision, which only considers their area of expertise.

Regulation writers at the Environmental Protection Agency, for example, usually think only about the environment. Those who toil at the IRS focus on regulations elaborating the tax code. The men and women who work for the Occupational Safety and Health Administration (OSHA) focus primarily on workplace issues. But rarely do these bureaucrats consider the overall good of the country or even the impact of their newly minted regulations on the larger economy and on preserving American jobs.

Obama's administration has produced new regulations at a record pace. During his first term alone, the feds issued 13,000 new regulations — a pace of about ten per day. And, in his second term, the regulation writers have run amok.

No congressional approval is required for new regulations or for changes in existing regulations. Some have proposed a federal regulatory budget that would fix the total cost of federal regulations at a set amount. Before any agency could add to the total, it would have to delete some other equally burdensome regulation. But there has been no progress along these lines in the Obama administration.

The chapters that follow deal with the various spheres of Obama's regulatory reach: health care, education, energy, environment, communications, and welfare. They track the dramatic expansion of the federal regulatory reach since 2009.

And all these new measures have one thing in common: They were not approved by Congress.

ObamaCare: The Biggest Power Grab of All — The Law That Means Anything They Say It Does

I F THERE IS ONE single Obama administration policy that unmistakably illustrates its ill-conceived strategy to ignore Congress and legislate on its own, it is, without a doubt, ObamaCare. The outlandish and autocratic process of ramming it through Congress and the disastrous way it was implemented speaks volumes. ObamaCare was — and is — the ultimate power grab.

If you want to understand what's wrong with Obama's plan to go it alone, go no further. A review of everything we know about ObamaCare tells the full story.

The arrogance, the incompetence, the deceitfulness, the over-reaching, and the scheming intrusiveness of Obama and his cronies were so transparently on display as the White House and the Department of Health and Human Services imploded in front of all of us. And it wasn't just the website fiasco that made it impossible for people to sign up for months after the launch. The problems were systemic.

It really shouldn't have been so surprising. ObamaCare had been heading for disaster since the beginning. The ObamaCare bill steamrolled through Congress in late 2009; it was rubber-stamped by top-heavy, democratic majorities in both houses who colluded with the Obama administration to keep it under wraps until the very last minute.

When the bill was finally brought to the House for a floor vote, most members had not been given adequate time to read it, let alone understand it. The bill was rushed through and its terms remained hush-hush until right before the vote. It was no better in the Senate. When then Senator Jim DeMint complained that he only had twenty-four hours to review a 3500-page bill, Democratic Senator Dick Durbin lashed back at him:

> For 46 hours and 8 minutes, the senator from South Carolina has had an opportunity to go to the Internet and see this bill in its entirety with the staff and read every page. For this senator to suggest on the floor that we are sneaking this bill, people haven't had a chance to see it, I would just say to the senator from South Carolina, welcome to the world of the Internet.[1]

By Durbin's terms, the Senators apparently had plenty of time to leisurely review the 3500-page ObamaCare bill, understand its implications, and verify its conclusions. A bill that suddenly regulated more than 17 percent of our GDP,[2] according to the World Health Organization, was obviously going to be challenging. Think about the enormity of it.

But Durbin pompously insisted that forty-six hours on the Internet was more than sufficient time to review it. Consider what he was suggesting. Within that time frame, assuming no sleep at all and doing absolutely nothing else for two days,

Senators only needed to read a little more than seventy pages an hour of a highly technical bill in order to struggle through it. If they slept about six hours each night, that number of pages per hour jumped to one hundred. Of course that left no time for tracking down answers to any questions — or even commuting to work, let alone discussing the provisions of the bill with constituents, colleagues, and, heaven forbid, the industries and people targeted by the bill. Does than seem more than a little absurd? Of course it does! That's why most members of Congress really didn't know exactly what they were voting on. Welcome to the Dick Durbin world of the Internet!

And it wasn't just a few people who didn't get it. Even Nancy Pelosi, the Speaker of the House at the time, was apparently unfamiliar with the bill's content. Her now famous comment made that pretty evident: "But we have to pass the bill so that you can find out what is in it . . ." she said.[3]

Huh?

Several years later, when ObamaCare had already been exposed as an indisputable fiasco, Pelosi unsuccessfully tried to explain her nutty remark to David Gregory. Try to figure this one out:

David Gregory: "And hasn't that idea, that you have to pass it before you know what's in it, isn't that really the problem, as you look back on it? That the — there was such a rush to get this done, no Republicans voting for it, and now there are unintended effects of this that were foreseen at the time that you couldn't know the impact of it. And now this is coming home to roost."

Rep. Nancy Pelosi: "No. What I was saying there is we are House and the Senate. We get a bill. We go to conference or we ping-pong it, and then you see what the final product is. However, I stand by what I said there. When people see what is in the bill, they will like it. And they will. And so, while there's a lot of hoop-di-doo and ado about what's happening now — very appropriate. I'm not criticizing. I'm saying it took a great deal for us to pass this bill. I said if we go up to the gate and the gate is locked, we'll unlock the gate. If we can't do that, we'll climb the fence. If the fence is too high, we'll pole vault in. If we can't do that, we'll helicopter in, but we'll get it done."[4]

All this Washington-speak about gates, fences, helicopters and whatever else is a bit confusing. Bottom line: Nancy had no idea what she was talking about — and she wasn't alone.

About the only thing everyone did immediately understand was that the ObamaCare bill was not at all understandable. If the Speaker didn't get it and members of Congress didn't get it, how were the voters who were kept completely in the dark supposed to get it? They didn't; they, too, were aghast at its complexity and confusion.

A Regulatory Nightmare

While the ObamaCare bill certainly didn't earn points for either its coherence or effectiveness, it did receive singular attention for one thing: its sheer size. Imagine . . . that's the one thing that distinguished this historic bill: its size.

With the final conference bill weighing in at 961 pages — 397 words to the page — totaled 381,517 words, according to the Government Printing Office.[5]

That was just the beginning, but we should have been forewarned. That should have been the first clue that ObamaCare was going to be a problem. If the best thing that could be said about it was that it was big, we were in trouble.

ObamaCare ultimately evolved into an open invitation to the bureaucratic regulation writers to gleefully work overtime setting up rules for every aspect of our nation's health care system, as well as our personal access to health care policies. It personified red tape gone wild.

According to CBS News, by mid-October 2013, after 109 "final" ObamaCare rules were published by the administration, they came to 10,535 pages, or about 12 million words.[6]

Again, 109 regulations!

By the end of 2013, *The Washington Post* reported that the regulatory mountain had grown to more than 20,000 pages — a pile taller than basketball star Kobe Bryant.[7]

Other than their height and weight, the regulations did little to improve the clarity of the bewildering legislation. The regulations were sloppy, filled with errors, and, in many cases, downright ridiculous. A study by the conservative American Action Forum reported that "a third of all the Obamacare regulations contained errors, forcing the administration to issue hundreds of corrections."[8] In the rush to get them out before the law's official launch on October 1, 2013, many of the regulations were approved with only a cursory review.

But errors were not the biggest problem. The real difficulty was that the regulations bore little resemblance to the law passed by Congress. Indeed, in many cases, they directly contradicted the actual text of the legislation Congress passed. The Obama functionaries at the Department of Health and Human Services (HHS) amended the law on their own, without consulting Congress, and in many cases, without consulting the industries and constituents who were most affected by the new requirement. The result was a sea of new rules that didn't make sense.

In fact, the most serious changes so fundamentally altered the law that it became an unrecognizable progeny of the original legislation, directly countering one of its most important provisions — the very public promise by the president of the United States that ObamaCare would not force you to change your existing health care plan.

Biggest Political Lie Ever

"If You Like Your Health Care Plan, You Can Keep Your Health Care Plan."

Sound familiar? Those fourteen words have become perhaps both the most famous and the most damaging phrase ever uttered by President Obama.

Over and over he repeated it. Over and over again, voters believed him, hoped in him. Until they found out it was one deliberate lie that was repeated over and over again.

It wasn't just Obama who peddled the big lie. Former HHS Secretary Kathleen Sebelius routinely promised what she knew to be untrue. And here's a list of twenty-seven democratic senators who repeated the same false tale:

- Sen. Harry Reid (D-NV)
- Sen. Richard Durbin (D-IL)
- Sen. Chuck Schumer (D-NY)
- Sen. Patty Murray (D-WA)
- Sen. Max Baucus (D-MT)
- Sen. Tom Harkin (D-IA)
- Then-Rep. Tammy Baldwin (D-WI)
- Sen. Mark Begich (D-AK)
- Sen. Michael Bennet (D-CO)
- Sen. Barbara Boxer (D-CA)
- Sen. Sherrod Brown (D-OH)
- Sen. Ben Cardin (D-MD)
- Sen. Kay Hagan (D-NC)
- Sen. Mary Landrieu (D-LA)
- Sen. Pat Leahy (D-VT)

- Sen. Bob Menendez (D-NJ)
- Sen. Jeff Merkley (D-OR)
- Sen. Barbara Mikulski (MD)
- Sen. Jay Rockefeller (D-WY)
- Sen. Jack Reed (D-RI)
- Sen. Bernie Sanders (I-VT)
- Sen. Jeanne Shaheen (D-NH)
- Sen. Debbie Stabenow (D-MI)
- Sen. Jon Tester (D-MT)
- Sen. Tom Udall (D-NM)
- Sen. Sheldon Whitehouse (D-RI)[9]

It all started with an op-ed piece that Obama wrote for *The New York Times* on August 15, 2009:

> If you don't have health insurance, you will finally have quality, affordable options once we pass reform. If you do have health insurance, we will make sure that no insurance company or government bureaucrat gets between you and the care you need. If you like your doctor, you can keep your doctor. If you like your health care plan, you can keep your health care plan. You will not be waiting in any lines. This is not about putting the government in charge of your health insurance. I don't believe anyone should be in charge of your health care decisions but you and your doctor — not government bureaucrats; not insurance companies.[10]

It sounded great, but it just wasn't true. When cancellation notices started raining down on more than 5 million Americans whose individual policies failed to pass HHS muster, one newspaper dubbed it the "lie of the year."[11]

That's some award!

We now know that Obama knew it was a lie every time he said it. Because, way back in 2010, HHS had projected millions of cancellations and quietly published its projections in the Federal Register inside a mass of regulation data that no one noticed.

Here's the thing: when the original ObamaCare bill passed, it clearly provided that preexisting policies would not be canceled. In fact, the law guaranteed it. The ObamaCare statute clearly stated that anyone who had a health insurance plan that was in effect on March 23, 2010, could keep it and not have it canceled, unless it had been significantly changed since then. That seemingly uncomplicated last phrase is where the problems began.

It became anything but uncomplicated as Obama and democratic politicians danced around it and then went into damage control.

It was the clear intent of the Congress that the grandfathered plans would not be canceled unless they had been gutted in the interim. At issue was how much the policy could be changed and still remain in force, grandfathered in.

On June 14, 2010, then HHS Secretary Kathleen Sebelius announced that the agency would be quite tolerant of changes in individual policies, saying "employers or issuers offering such coverage will have the flexibility of making reasonable changes without losing their 'grandfathered' status."[12]

Sebelius even gave examples of where the borderline might be drawn: "However, if health plans significantly raise co-payments or deductibles, or if they significantly reduce benefits — for example, if they stop covering treatment for a disease like HIV/AIDS or cystic fibrosis — they'll lose their grandfathered status and their customers will get the same full set of consumer protections as new plans."[13]

Believe it or not, Sebelius then went on to repeat the Obama mantra: "Bottom line is that under the Affordable Care Act, if you like your doctor and plan, you can keep them."[14]

The truth was that it was unlikely if you could keep either.

If we let this lie stand — without holding Obama accountable — democracy will have lost its most vital feature: accountability. First, in the 2014 congressional elections, then in the 2016 presidential election, we must put Obama's big lie front and center. It must be our battle cry.

HHS Orders the Cancellation of Millions of Health Care Policies

Deep inside the Department of Health and Human Services, the bureaucrats had something very different in mind. The regulations they ultimately issued provided that virtually *any* change in a policy held by individuals would make it ineligible for grandfather status. The plans would be canceled. The promised flexibility went out the window.

As a result, 4.8 million Americans who held individual health care coverage, received cancellation notices[15] because of changes in their plans. Not changes they objected to. Nor changes that they didn't want. No, *any* change whatsoever triggered a cancellation.

Even Obama acted surprised. He told NBC "I am sorry that they are finding themselves in this situation based on assurances they got from me." He promised to "work hard to make sure that they know we hear them and we are going to do everything we can to deal with folks who find themselves in a tough position as a consequence of this."[16]

Even as he apologized, the White House insisted that he had not misled anyone.

One major Democrat, House Minority Whip, Steny Hoyer, disagreed with Carney, however slightly. Hoyer admitted that the president's message "was not precise enough." . . . [it] should have been caveated with — 'Assuming you have a policy that, in fact, does do what the bill is designed to do.'"[17]

Does that sound at all like what the president and his Democratic Party minions peddled more than fifty times? At the time, it was hard to understand why HHS and the insurance companies doing its bidding had seemingly gone berserk, canceling any policy in sight. But the answer turned out to be very simple. It was because the very premise of ObamaCare required it. The health care legislation was essentially a scheme to tax Americans who have insurance to pay for those that don't. But, unwilling to impose a real tax, ObamaCare demanded that those with insurance dig deeper into their pockets to pay for more comprehensive coverage, even if they don't need it and don't want it. The goal was not to give them broader coverage. It's to justify the higher premiums that the government and participating insurance companies must collect so that they have money to subsidize the coverage of the currently uninsured.

The simple fact is that if everybody who liked their health care plan chose to keep it, as Obama had assured them they could, there would be no surplus revenue to cover the uninsured and ObamaCare would fail for lack of revenues.

And Obama knew that.

There was another reason for the HHS-induced cancellation of existing health insurance plans: ObamaCare desperately needed young and healthy people to insure.

Because unless a high percentage of those getting covered by ObamaCare were young and healthy, the risk pool would be too old and too sick, driving up premiums to unaffordable levels and dooming the plan. So the program needed to throw millions of healthy and young people out of their current plans to force them to enter the ObamaCare risk pool to keep it young and lower its costs.

That's what it was all about.

There's no question that Obama knew all of this when he made his phony pledge that people could keep their health insurance. He knew he was lying. He knew that the theory behind his program required that they lose their policies. But he blatantly lied to get the bill passed. It's as simple as that.

And the Senators and Representatives who voted for the bill also knew it was a lie, but they were caught between two imperatives:

a. ObamaCare couldn't pass unless they assured those with health policies that they could keep them; and

b. Obamacare couldn't work unless the policies were, in fact, canceled.

So once the ink was dry on Obama's signature on March 23, 2010, it fell to the HHS bureaucrats to unobtrusively make things right by enacting rules that forced the cancellation of the very policies Obama and his legislative minions had pledged to preserve. Lisa Myers of NBC News reported that three and a half years before ObamaCare went into effect, HHS issued a regulation estimating that "because of the normal turnover in the individual insurance market "40 to 67 percent of customers will not be able to keep their policies."[18]

So, while President Obama was promising that everyone who liked their policies could keep them, HHS was predicting that most of the individual policies in the US would be canceled!

When challenged about the numbers and about the president's awareness of this disaster, White House Press Secretary Jay Carney dismissed it as involving only 5 percent of the population – or 15 million people.[19]

Only 15 million people?

But it was much worse than that. *Forbes* reported that:

'The Department's mid-range estimate is that 66 percent of small employer plans and 45 percent of large employer plans will relinquish their grandfather status by the end of 2013.' According to the Congressional Budget Office, 156 million Americans — more than half the population — were covered by employer-sponsored insurance in 2013.[20]

According to *Forbes*, the blockbuster estimates were buried in a June 2010 edition of the *Federal Register*.

A staggering 45 and 66 percent?!

Once the public outrage hit the fan, however, all bets were off. So outraged were the American people by Obama's lie that his ratings immediately plunged. The CNN poll of November 2013 found that 53 percent said the president was not "honest and trustworthy."[21]

Obama quickly backtracked. Using the royal "we," he claimed to have said something completely different:

"What we said was you can keep it if it hasn't changed since the law passed."[22]

This was a stunning repudiation of the statement that Obama had made at least 36 times on video! *The Washington Free Beacon* compiled a summary video of these unequivocal promises. Go to https://www.youtube.com/watch?v=qpa-5JdCnmo.

Take a look. It's sickening!

National Journal's Ron Fournier reported that *The Washington Post* awarded the president "four Pinocchios for the 'you-can-keep-it' lie, repeated countless times by Obama . . . The White House now cites technicalities to avoid admitting that he went too far in his repeated pledge, which, after all, is one of the most famous statements of his presidency."[23] (Four Pinocchios, the worst designation, is reserved for "whoppers.")

Fournier also noted the presidential body language when Obama was eventually caught in his lie and started to backpedal — he was reading from prepared notes, not making eye contact, in an obviously "orchestrated deceit."[24] And Obama was still touting his 'you can keep your policy' lie in 2012 — two years *after* his own administration announced it was most unlikely! Something had to give. Senate Democrats, up for reelection in 2014, demanded that the president act to rescind the cancellations, no matter what the law said.

And Obama obliged. Once again, he unilaterally changed the law, without the authority to do so. On November 14, 2013, he announced that insurance companies would have the option of continuing existing health care plans for one year, even if they had changed, if the company chose to do so and if the state insurance commissioner allowed it to be done.[25]

Isn't this precious? If the state insurance commissioner approves and the insurance company agrees, the law — as passed by Congress — will be enforced. If not, the bureaucratic regulations, which go counter to the language and intent of the statute — will have to prevail.

So much for the rule of law.

As it turned out, many state insurance commissioners, particularly those in democratic states, chose to bar reconsideration of the cancellations, forcing them to proceed. The Obama administration's need to make the risk pool younger and healthier prevailed over the plain meaning of the statute as it had been passed by Congress — to say nothing of the wishes of their constituents to keep their health care plans.

As a result of the ideological fidelity of the state insurance commissioners in blue states, many policyholders still faced cancellation despite Obama's attempted reprieve. Pressure mounted for more action. The House passed a bill requiring the rescission of the cancellations, in effect, passing a bill to reiterate what it had already said in the ObamaCare bill.

So just before Christmas in 2013, Obama caved in once again and announced that the five million individual policyholders whose health care plans had been canceled would not need to buy new health insurance at all — despite the law's requirement that they do so — and that they would also be exempt from the fines the law imposed for not having any insurance. He also backed down on the ban on buying special catastrophic policies for people over thirty, policies that previously had only been available to people under the age of thirty.[26]

Once again, Obama and his people interpreted the Affordable Care Act to mean anything they say it means. And, once again, they did this without the legal authority to do so and without the consent of Congress. Of course, Obama's retreats on the cancellation of policies taken out by individuals raises the question of what will happen to those who get their health care policies through their employers, particularly through small- and medium-sized employers. Legally, the same standards apply to these group policy holders as governed individual policies: If the policy has been changed since 2010, it will be canceled.

Since the pool of those covered under group plans is about twenty times larger than those in individual plans, the mayhem that will result from the massive cancellations will dwarf the reaction of the 5 million who had been canceled by the end of 2013.

Will Obama retreat again? Will the Affordable Care Act again mean whatever Obama says it will mean?

The Bottom Line: Only 2.6 Million Previously Uninsured Americans Signed Up and Paid For ObamaCare[27]

Although Obama and the Democrats had relentlessly promised that 36 million uninsured Americans would be covered by ObamaCare, it turned out to be a vast overestimate. As of mid-April 2014, the White House claimed that 8 million people were signed up.[28] But, according to McKinsey, only 26 percent of those who actually signed up and paid for a premium were previously uninsured[29] — that's slightly more than *2 million people*. And those 2 million are only 5.5 percent of the 36 million uninsured that Obama persistently claimed would be covered. The single most cited reason for the decision not to buy insurance was the cost, according to a poll by the Kaiser Family Foundation.[30]

So, it turns out that The Affordable Health Care Act is . . . unaffordable.

The Law Says Whatever We Say It Says

In addition to illegally modifying, changing, revising, and deleting sections of ObamaCare that were passed by Congress, HHS has, on at least one occasion, actually interpreted the Affordable Care Act to mean the exact opposite of what it says in its text.

If that's not legislating on your own, nothing is. The most egregious example became the basis of a lawsuit brought by the State of Oklahoma in federal court.

The Affordable Care Act quite specifically limits federal subsidies for health insurance premiums to those receiving their coverage through *state-created* insurance exchanges. The exact language of the statute states that subsidies are available to people who buy insurance "through an Exchange established by the State."[31] At the time the bill was passed, the administration assumed that each state would set up its own exchange, relieving Washington of the burden of having to doing so. But, surprisingly, thirty-four states opted not to create exchanges,[32] so Washington had to step in and set them up for them.

The statute was silent about giving subsidies to people who get their policies through *federal* as opposed to *state* exchanges. So the only language to rely on was the language about the availability to the states. But the IRS, in writing the rule to implement the law's subsidies, made no distinction whatsoever between state-established exchanges and federal ones, ruling, instead, that subsidies were available to anyone regardless of who set up the exchange.

Oklahoma Attorney General Scott Pruitt disagreed with the Obama administration's creative, but improper, interpretation. Pruitt sued, alleging his state had never created any exchange and, therefore, people in Oklahoma were not eligible for subsidies. These subsidies lie at the very heart of the ObamaCare program. The law sets such a high bar for comprehensive coverage that the insurance plans are bound to be very expensive. So the subsidies are crucial. Without them, the law's requirement that everybody buy insurance is unsupportable and the entire edifice collapses. That's why Congress made subsidies available to people whose income is below four times the poverty level ($95,400 for a family of four [2014]). But if the subsidies can only be paid to those covered through state exchanges, the law collapses completely.

But that's what the law says in plain black and white.

In a similar case, US District Court Judge Paul Friedman, appointed by Bill Clinton and sitting in DC, rejected a challenge to the ObamaCare subsidies similar to that which Pruitt is bringing in Oklahoma. Judge Friedman said that Act indicated intent to provide sweeping coverage.

"[T]here is evidence throughout the statute of Congress's desire to ensure broad access to affordable health coverage," the judge wrote, upholding subsidies for those covered through federal exchanges.[33]

The case, *Halbig v. Sebelius* is on appeal, but the Pruitt case is separate and will be adjudicated first by the Oklahoma US District Court. George Will contends that the legislative intent discerned by Judge Friedman is not so clear. And constitutional scholar John Adler seriously disagrees. Will notes that:

In Senate Finance Committee deliberations on the ACA, Chairman Max Baucus (D-MT), one of the bill's primary authors, suggested the possibility of conditioning tax credits on state compliance because only by doing so could the federal government induce state cooperation with the ACA. Then the law's insurance requirements could be imposed on states without running afoul of constitutional law precedents that prevent the federal government from commandeering state governments. The pertinent language originated in the committee and was clarified in the Senate.[34]

Will the Court allow Obama not only to interpret the law as he pleases, but to contravene its clear text? So far, that's what's happening, but there's much more to come. We will see.

Obama Can Change the Law Anytime He Wants

President Obama has treated the Affordable Care Act as his own personal piece of legislation, written by his people, sold by his own words, and adopted by his rubber-stamp majorities in Congress.

But along with pride of authorship and sensitivity to criticism has come another kind of strange ownership of the law — a distorted sense that he can unilaterally alter it and even contradict its plain language anytime he feels it advisable — without asking Congress and without any legal authority. More than two dozen times, he has substantially changed the law on his own, in cahoots with his bureaucratic enablers at the Department of Health and Human Services.

He's truly operating on his own!

Some of the modifications satisfied criticisms and objections to the law. Some satisfied his constituents; others gave ground to its opponents. Others amplified the effect of the law. Still more postponed key parts of it. But one thing all had in common: The president had no business making the changes on his own. His job, according to the Constitution is to "take care that the laws be faithfully enforced" (Article II Section 3) — not to interpret them anyway he chooses.

Listed below are twenty-two material changes in the Affordable Care Act that President Obama has promulgated by executive action without consultation with Congress, chronicled by Tyler Hartsfield and Grace-Marie Turner of the Galen Institute. They read like the actions of a dictator who doesn't consult with anyone when he writes the laws.

Unilateral Changes in Affordable Care Act Made By President Obama:Changes By Administrative Action[35]

1. **Medicare Advantage patch:** The *administration ordered an advance draw* on funds from a Medicare bonus program in

order to provide extra payments to Medicare Advantage plans in an effort to temporarily forestall cuts in benefits and therefore delay early exodus of MA plans from the program. (April 19, 2011)

2. **Employee reporting:** The administration, contrary to the ObamaCare legislation, *instituted a one-year delay* of the requirement that employers must report to their employees on their W-2 forms the full cost of their employer-provided health insurance. (January 1, 2012)

3. **Subsidies may flow through federal exchanges:** The *IRS issued an ambiguous rule* that allows premium assistance tax credits to be available in federal exchanges, although the law only specified that they would be available "through an Exchange established by the State under Section 1311." (May 23, 2012)

4. **Delaying a low-income plan:** The *administration delayed implementation of the Basic Health Program* until 2015. It would have provided more affordable health coverage for certain low-income individuals not eligible for Medicaid. (February 7, 2013)

5. **Closing the high-risk pool:** The *administration decided to halt enrollment* in transitional federal high-risk pools created by the law, blocking coverage for an estimated 40,000 new applicants, citing a lack of funds. The administration had money from a fund under Secretary Sebelius's control to extend the pools, but instead used the money to pay for advertising for ObamaCare enrollment and other purposes. (February 15, 2013)

6. **Doubling allowed deductibles:** Because some group health plans use more than one benefits administrator, plans are allowed to apply separate patient cost-sharing limits for

one year to different services, such as doctor/hospital and prescription drugs, allowing maximum out-of-pocket costs to be twice as high as the law intended. (February 20, 2013)

7. **Small businesses on hold:** The administration has said that the federal exchanges for small businesses will not be ready by the 2014 statutory deadline, and instead *delayed until 2015 the provision of SHOP* (Small-Employer Health Option Program) that requires the exchanges to offer a choice of qualified health plans. (March 11, 2013)

8. **Employer-mandate delay:** By an administrative action that's contrary to statutory language in the ACA, the *reporting requirements for employers were delayed by one year.* (July 2, 2013)

9. **Self-attestation:** Because of the difficulty of verifying income *after the employer-reporting requirement was delayed, the administration decided it would allow "self-attestation" of income* by applicants for health insurance in the exchanges. This was later partially retracted after congressional and public outcry over the likelihood of fraud. (July 15, 2013)

10. **Delaying the online SHOP exchange:** The administration first *delayed* the October 1, 2013, launch of the online, small-business insurance exchange for a month, then delayed once more for a year, until November 2014. (September 26, 2013; November 27, 2013)

11. **Congressional opt-out:** The a*dministration decided to offer employer contributions to members of Congress* and their staffs when they purchase insurance on the exchanges created by the ACA, a subsidy the law doesn't provide. (September 30, 2013)

12. **Delaying the individual mandate:** The *administration changed the deadline for the individual mandate* by declaring

that customers who have purchased insurance by March 31, 2014, will avoid the tax penalty. Previously, they would have had to purchase a plan by mid-February. (October 23, 2013)

13. **Insurance companies may offer canceled plans:** The administration announced that insurance companies may *reoffer plans that previous regulations forced them to cancel.* (November 14, 2013)

14. **Exempting unions from reinsurance fee:** The administration gave unions an *exemption* from the reinsurance fee (one of ObamaCare's many new taxes). To make up for this exemption, *non-exempt plans will have to pay a higher fee, which will likely be passed onto consumers* in the form of higher premiums and deductibles. (December 2, 2013)

15. **Extending Preexisting Condition Insurance Plan:** The administration *extended the federal high risk pool until January 31, 2014,* and again until *March 15, 2014,* and again until *April 30, 2014,* to prevent a coverage gap for the most vulnerable. The plans were scheduled to expire on December 31, but were extended because it has been impossible for some to sign up for new coverage on Healthcare.gov. (December 12, 2013; January 14, 2014; March 14, 2014)

16. **Expanding hardship waiver to those with canceled plans:** The administration *expanded the hardship waiver, which excludes people from the individual mandate* and allows some to purchase catastrophic health insurance — who have had their plans canceled because of ObamaCare regulations. The administration later *extended* this waiver until October 1, 2016. (December 19, 2013) (March 5, 2014)

17. **Equal employer coverage delayed:** Tax officials *will not be enforcing in 2014 the mandate requiring employers to offer equal coverage to all their employees.* This provision of the law was supposed to go into effect in 2010, but IRS officials have "yet to issue regulations for employers to follow." (January 18, 2014)

18. **Employer-mandate delayed again:** The *administration delayed for an additional year provisions of the employer mandate,* postponing enforcement of the requirement for medium-sized employers until 2016 and relaxing some requirements for larger employers. Businesses with 100 or more employees must offer coverage to 70 percent of their full-time employees in 2015 and 95 percent in 2016 and beyond. (February 10, 2014)

19. **Extending subsidies to non-exchange plans:** The administration released a bulletin through the Centers for Medicare & Medicaid Services (CMS) *extending subsidies to individuals who purchased health insurance plans outside* of the federal or state exchanges. The bulletin *also requires retroactive coverage and subsidies for individuals from the date they applied on the marketplace rather than the date they actually enrolled in a plan.* The Congressional Research Service (CRS) issued a memo discussing the legality of these subsidies. (February 27, 2014)

20. **Non-compliant health plans get two-year extension:** The *administration pushed back the deadline by two years that requires health insurers to cancel plans* that are not compliant with ObamaCare's mandates. These "illegal" plans may now be offered until 2017. This extension will prevent a wave cancellation notices from going out before the 2014 midterm elections. (March 5, 2014)

21. **Delaying the sign-up deadline:** The *administration delayed until mid-April the March 31 deadline to sign up for insurance.* Applicants simply need to check a box on their application to qualify for this extended sign-up period. (March 26, 2014)

22. **Canceling Medicare Advantage cuts:** The administration canceled scheduled cuts to Medicare Advantage. The *ACA calls for $200 billion in cuts to Medicare Advantage over 10 years.* (April 7, 2014)

Were the Affordable Care Act passed by a hostile Congress over the president's veto, Obama's reinterpretation of its provisions would be understandable. But *he* wrote the law! It was his hand that set it in place. The changes are the acts of an arrogant president who believes America is a nation led by men, not by laws.

Big Labor Talks and Obama Jumps

As discussed earlier, one of the motivations for Obama's power grab has been to pander to his liberal constituents. That was all too evident in his actions on ObamaCare.

The Affordable Care Act requires all employers of more than fifty full time workers to offer them health insurance policies or to pay a steep fine, beginning at $2,000 per employee. The provision had the perverse effect of stimulating part-time employment. The ObamaCare statute defined "full-time" work as more than thirty hours per week. Consequently, companies began to recast their workforces to shift more people to part-time jobs to get in under the fifty full-time jobs threshold for mandatory health insurance. The trend soon became a stampede.

Keith Hall, the director of the Bureau of Labor Statistics from 2008 to 2012, notes that in the first six months of 2013, 97 percent of the new jobs created were part-time. He called the trend "really remarkable."[36] Of 963,000 more people who reported to the Bureau that they were employed, 936,000 were in part-time jobs.[37]

"That is a really high number for a six-month period," Hall said. "I'm not sure that has ever happened over six months before."[38]

In fact, in 2012, almost 90 percent of the jobs created were full-time. But in 2013, 90 percent were part-time. Obviously, the perverse incentives of ObamaCare were mainly at fault. The surge in part-time work left many very unhappy, especially among labor union leaders. AFL-CIO President Richard Trumka was particularly upset. He charged that "employers are trying to plan their future by creating a work force that gets twenty-nine-and-a-half hours or less a week so they don't have to pay for health care." Trumka admitted to being surprised by the trend: "That is obviously something that no one intended. No one intended for an act to be the result of people working fewer hours, just so they [employers] don't have to pay for health care, so that's something that needs to be addressed. Is that an issue? Yeah, that's an issue."[39]

When big labor talks, big government listens. And the Obama White House is the big government of all big governments. That's why, on July 2, 2013, President Obama announced that he was delaying the requirement that businesses provide health insurance to their full-time workers for one year, until the start of 2015.

Did the law allow him to do so? No.

Did the Affordable Care Act require the mandate on employers to take effect at the start of 2014? Yes.

Did Obama care? No. Not one bit.

Fighting Back the Power Grab

Obama's power grab rests on two pillars: his one arrogant tendency toward usurpation, and the Senate's supine compliance in going along with him. In 2014 and 2016, we must destroy both of these pillars and bring down the house. In 2014, we must capture the Senate, but it will not be until 2016, when we elect a new president, that we will be able to restore the system of checks and balances to our country.

Congressman Tom Rice (R-SC) cared about the rule of law. He held the naive impression that the president was supposed to carry out the laws, not amend them unilaterally and retroactively. In December of 2013, Rice and twenty-nine other Republican Congressmen introduced a House resolution proposing that the chamber sue President Obama to force him to follow the law and implement the employer mandate on schedule.

The resolution noted that Obama has shown a "continuing failure to faithfully execute"[40] several laws. In addition to challenging the delay in the employer mandate, Rice is also seeking to stop Obama from rescinding the cancellation of individual health insurance plans. The big problem the House would face in such a lawsuit, according to Peter M. Shane, a professor of law at the Ohio State University, would be whether Congress had the standing to bring the lawsuit. Could the House prove that it was sufficiently injured by the delay to give it the standing to sue?[41]

That's not a problem for Dr. Larry Kawa, a Florida dentist, who says that he spent thousands of dollars in anticipation of having to cover all his employees and is now left holding the bag. Represented by the conservative legal action group Judicial Watch, he has sued the administration, saying that the president has no authority "to pick and choose which parts of the law he's going to enforce for the sake of political convenience."[42]

Unlike so many who opposed the unilateral changes Obama has made in health care, Kawa claimed to have standing as a result of his economic losses. His lawsuit was dismissed by the US District Court in Florida on standing issues, but he has appealed and expects a decision very soon.

Congressman Jim Gerlach (R-PA) has another approach in mind. He has introduced legislation to give either chamber of Congress automatic standing to bring challenges to either executive branch usurpation of power for its failure to follow the Constitutional requirement that the president "take care that the laws be *faithfully* executed"[43] The Gerlach bill would give such lawsuits a fast track to the Supreme Court for adjudication.

His bill makes sense. If a majority of one house of Congress feels the president is out of line, it should be able to get a hearing by the Supreme Court without either having to hunt for a suitable plaintiff or to wait for years for a case to work its way up in the courts. The delays a challenger to Obama's executive branch usurpations faces are formidable. A challenge to his 2010 recess appointments to the National Labor Relations Board (appointments made when Congress is in recess that are, therefore, not subject to Senate confirmation) was not heard by the Supreme Court until 2014 after a long and largely successful voyage through the lower courts.

Obama Exempts Congress from ObamaCare

When ObamaCare was advancing through Congress, its Republican opponents assaulted the measure with all kinds of amendments to weaken its requirements. One of the few that got passed and made it into the law was introduced by Senator Chuck Grassley (R-IA) requiring all members of Congress and their staffs to get their health care through the same exchanges as they were setting up for the rest of the country.

But no sooner did the law take effect than the Obama administration waived the offensive provision and carved out an exemption for members of Congress, although it was the precise opposite of the explicit provision of the law itself. And Obama did it without asking Congress to vote on the repeal of the provision.

That was a serious power grab. Obama seized one section of a legitimate statute and in one illegal stroke, eliminated it. Eliminating the will of Congress, and eliminating something his cronies objected to but could not afford to defeat in Congress. Because members of Congress would not have looked good if they publicly argued against applying the same exact terms to themselves as the rest of the country. They didn't want to be stuck with ObamaCare, but they couldn't afford to openly take a stand against it. But deep down they knew the real issue: Why should they be treated like just regular folks?

So they kept quiet, knowing that their friend in the White House would rescue them. Obama understood completely. Elites in each branch of government speak the same self-serving language.

Here's how it happened: Senate Democrats came to the president, hat in hand, desperate to repeal the provision applying ObamaCare to them. Under their current cushy deal, members of Congress get their insurance through the federal government. Washington obligingly picks up 75 percent of the tab for the coverage.

But if the members had to get their coverage through the exchanges, they would not be eligible for any subsidy. (Remember: Subsidies are only available for those making four times the poverty level. Members of Congress get paid $174,000 a year[44] — more than ten times the poverty level. ObamaCare exchanges do not allow tax-exempt employer contributions to health care premiums. The only subsidies available to individuals on ObamaCare are the premium tax credits for individuals who are under 400 percent of the federal poverty line.[45]

Democrats wanted to continue to get the subsidy, but did not want to have to vote for it, certain that it would be used against them when they ran for reelection. So Obama exempted them with the stroke of a pen — no Congressional action required; no telltale votes for opponents to use against them.

How did Obama manage that one? He ruled that senators and representatives did have to go through the exchanges as the law provided, but he directed his Office of Personnel Management (OPM) to rule that they would still be eligible for the 75 percent subsidy from the government. That's right. Members of

Congress and certain designated staff members were covered by this giveaway.

Not everybody in Congress agreed with the change. Senator Ron Johnson (R-WI) has sued to overturn the administration's action, saying that "by arranging for members of Congress and their staffs to receive benefits intentionally ruled out by the Patient Protection and Affordable Care Act, the administration has exceeded its legal authority."[46]

Johnson noted that:

> During the drafting, debate and passage of ObamaCare, the issue of how the law should affect members of Congress and their staffs was repeatedly addressed. Even a cursory reading of the legislative history clearly shows the intent of Congress was to ensure that members and staff would no longer be eligible for their current coverage under the Federal Employee Health Benefit Plan.[47]

So how did Obama manage to find a way for a federal agency — the OPM — to overrule a law passed by Congress? Johnson explains that the OPM "essentially declared the federal government a small employer — magically qualifying members of Congress for coverage through a Small Business Health Options Program, exchanges where employers can buy insurance for their employees."[48]

The House has repeatedly passed bills overturning the administration action and subjecting itself and the Senate to ObamaCare, without the subsidy. But the Senate has never done the same. Democrats are understandably horrified lest the law they passed apply to them!

President Obama is continuing to treat the Affordable Care Act as if it were still being drafted prior to congressional passage. We've discussed earlier former Speaker Nancy Pelosi's "hare-brained" comment that "we have to pass the bill so that you can find out what is in it."[49]

She was wrong!

Even now that Congress has passed this benighted piece of legislation, we still don't know what is in it. We have to wait for our president to decide what it says.

So what can we do about it? Can't the courts control Obama's abuse of executive law making? The lawsuits by the state of Oklahoma, Senator Ron Johnson, and Congressman Tom Rice may help. The courts may grant them standing to sue. Otherwise, the only ones who can sue are those who are directly injured by the administrations; action — narrow criteria that may handcuff the courts in making Obama follow the law he wrote and he got passed.

For now, he's grabbed all the power there is.

CHAPTER 2

Common Core Curriculum: Obama Federalizes Education To Dumb It Down

IF OBAMA'S CONSTITUENTS CANNOT make it through today's American public education system as it stands, he's determined to dumb it down so that they can. In a classic application of the diminution of standards that has accompanied such ill-fated liberal policies as affirmative action and open enrollment in the past, Obama is pushing the "Common Core Curriculum" to lower standards at both the K-12 and college levels. To accomplish this questionable goal, the Obama administration has overseen and promoted a revolutionary turnaround in the role of the federal government in education, which until now was largely a state function. Some have called it a blatant "power grab" by Washington, designed not only to take over the state's role in education, but also to reach into the classroom and carefully limit and manage the information that reaches each student.[1]

Stanley Kurtz, author of *Spreading the Wealth: How Obama is Robbing the Suburbs to Pay for the Cities*, points out how Obama virtually ignored Congress on this controversial issue, never even submitting this contentious education plan for review, preferring the alternative of targeting stimulus money for his pet project.[2] That strategy assured that there was no debate at all and also allowed him to secretly devise the core curriculum without those who are most affected by the change getting in the way.

Congress and parents need not apply.

It's become obvious that openness and forthrightness has been a consistent problem with Obama. According to the White House website, the president promised that his administration would be "the most open and transparent in history," but that has not been the case. In fact, an analysis by the Associated Press in 2014 revealed just the opposite. Instead of growing more transparent, the Obama administration "has grown more secretive over time, last year censoring or outright denying FOI [Freedom of Information] access to government files more than ever since Obama took office."[3] To Obama, transparency has become merely a figure of speech that does not apply to him. So it's not surprising that the Obama education reform, like ObamaCare, was conceived in the dark.

While the Obama administration describes Core Curriculum (sometimes derisively called "ObamaCore") as simply a set of voluntary national standards, Kurtz and others view them very differently and have criticized the political basis for the Core Curriculum as "the hard left's education agenda."[4] Kurtz identified the three controversial — and virtually unspoken — goals of the Common Core:

1. "a politicized curriculum that promotes leftist notions of 'social justice,'

2. reducing disparate outcomes between students in different districts by undercutting standards,

3. a redistribution of suburban education funding to less well-off urban schools."[5]

Is that what the innocuous-sounding program is really designed to achieve by interloping the federal government into local classrooms? Although the discreetly-devised program was initially accepted by most states, there is now loud criticism from both the left and the right that is leading to a new appraisal of the Common Core and its effectiveness, its invasion of students' privacy, and its underlying intent. And the entire concept of the Core Curriculum has raised serious questions about the relationship of the federal government to the states.

If there is one area of governance that has traditionally been the domain of state and local authorities, it is public education at the elementary, high school, and university levels. But that historic separation hasn't stopped Obama from intruding on long-established state prerogatives in his massive federal power grab. And it's not even based on the federal government's interest in how its money is spent. The federal contribution to state education is surprisingly low. Of the $600 billion spent in 2011, only $73.7 billion came from the federal government — a mere 12 percent.[6]

But that makes no difference to Obama. Wherever there's a vacuum, he sees an opportunity to seize state power and allocate it to the federal government — to grab power. And that's exactly what he's doing here.

The US Constitution makes no mention of education whatsoever. Because of that, there has always been an assumption that the Tenth Amendment, which reserves to the states all powers not specifically allocated to the federal government in the document itself, means that education is a state responsibility. And that's precisely what it's always been.

We must stop Obama from taking over our schools. It's bad enough that he grabs power over this generation, but we must stop him from taking over the schools that educate the next generation. This task makes a Republican victory in 2016 all the more imperative because when it comes to education, we are not just debating the present, we are determining our future.

But under Obama, the federal government is making a concerted effort to take it over by promoting what it calls "Common Core State Standards." Rachel Alexander, editor of the *Intellectual Conservative*, criticizes the goals of the Common Core that imposes national controls and "eliminates local control over K-12 curriculum in math and English, instead imposing a one-size-fits-all, top-down curriculum that will also apply to private schools and homeschoolers."[7]

The origin of the Common Core Curriculum is itself a subject of controversy, with its advocates pointing to its roots in state education groups, governors, and private education reform circles. Officially, the curriculum was originally drafted by state education superintendents working with the National Governors Association, with input from the American Federation of Teachers and the National Education Association, but its opponents suspect that the heavy lifting was left to the federal Department of Education. Any suggestion that the Common Core emerged from parents and grassroots groups is scoffed at by Diane Ravich, a respected former Assistant US Secretary of Education appointed by both President Bush-41 and President Bill Clinton. To the contrary, Ravich says that Common Core was developed "by an organization called 'Achieve' along with the National Governors Association, both of which were generously funded by the Gates Foundation. There was minimal public engagement in the development of the Common Core. Their creation was neither grassroots nor did it emanate from the states."[8]

Rachel Alexander seconds this view adding that common core is, indeed, "driven by policy makers in D.C."[9]

A cursory review of Achieve's website indicates that it is, in fact, dominated by big business, big business foundations, and well-known liberal foundations. Alcoa, Intel, Prudential, MetLife, ExxonMobil, State Farm, Boeing, Travelers, and Microsoft are paired with the Carnegie Corporation of New York, the Bill & Melinda Gates Foundation, and the AT&T Foundation.

Doesn't sound like the local PTAs were given much input, does it? So the leaders of big business and big foundations, none of whom have seen a classroom for a very long time, decided what their ideal national curriculum should be. And now that's federal policy.

Here's a list of Achieve's supporters found on its website:[10]

- Alcoa Foundation
- AT&T Foundation
- The Battelle Foundation
- Bill & Melinda Gates Foundation
- The Boeing Company
- Brookhill Foundation
- Carnegie Corporation of New York
- Chevron
- The Cisco Foundation
- DuPont
- ExxonMobil
- The GE Foundation
- GSK
- IBM Corporation
- Intel Foundation
- JP Morgan Chase Foundation
- The Joyce Foundation
- The Leona & Harry B. Helmsley Charitable Trust
- Lumina Foundation

- MetLife Foundation
- Microsoft
- Nationwide
- Noyce Foundation
- The Prudential Foundation
- S. D. Bechtel, Jr. Foundation
- Sandler Foundation
- State Farm Insurance Companies
- Travelers Foundation
- The William and Flora Hewlett Foundation

Not exactly the hoi polloi!

The business-based nature of this "education reform" has not been a big selling point with either the left or the right. Indeed, on May 8, 2014, the Chicago teachers union (a division of NEA, the National Education Association) voted to oppose the Common Core Curriculum. Union members focused on the source of the curricula, claiming that, "the standards better reflect the interests and priorities of corporate education reformers than the best interests and priorities of teachers and students."[11]

Dumbing Down Schools

The Common Core curriculum is not a broad policy statement about our education system. In fact, it's voluntary. But following it is mandatory if a start wants to get the big money available from the Department of Education. The Common Core Curriculum is a meddlesome directive specifying exactly how each teacher is to teach each subject to each class each day. Its prescriptions are precise and must be followed to the letter. The curriculum comes complete with diagnostic tests to measure how well teachers and schools are administering and teaching the curriculum. It certainly doesn't sound like a voluntary set of standards, does it?[12]

In a recent example, students at a Common Core school were asked to subtract 270 from 530. It was not enough to give the answer: 260. Students had to show how they derived it. One student, who did it the way we all learned to do arithmetic and came up with the right answer, was marked wrong because he didn't use the designated approved method. The Common Core curriculum wanted him to change 270 into the "friendly number" 300. Then subtract 300 from 530 and add back the 30 you lost when you changed 270 to the "friendly" 300, for a total of 260.[13]

That doesn't sound so friendly to us.

At a more advanced level, the math standards of Common Core do not permit elementary algebra to be taught until the 9th grade. By this move, subjects like calculus and trigonometry will not be taught in high school because, by the time the student takes geometry and intermediate and advanced algebra, it will be time to graduate. This requirement will, in turn, dumb down college math in the freshman year and force schools to teach calculus to beginners!

Mathematics professor J. James Milgram of Stanford University, and the only mathematician on the Common Core Validation Committee, refused to sign off on the math standards because they would put many students two years behind those of many high-achieving countries.[14]

When it comes to reading, the Common Core curriculum does not stress books, much less classics, but focuses instead on instructional manuals. Children read things like instructions on how to operate a lawn mower or how to fill in a tax form. Isn't that the very definition of dumbing down?

The American Principles Project stresses that Common Core "de-emphasizes the study of classic literature in favor of reading so-called 'informational texts such as government documents, court opinions and technical manuals.'"[15]

One observer noted that over half the reading materials in grades 6–12 are informational texts rather than classical literature.

Children are not to be taught cursive or script, but only print-ing. How they are to communicate with the rest of the adult population that uses cursive is left a mystery.

The standards for other subjects, apart from reading and math, have yet to be formulated, but they will doubtless embody the same sophistry as those we know about. Many people worry that the standards for history, civics, social studies, and English may smack of leftist ideology and serve as part of an effort to indoctrinate students.

The Department of Education has urged Common Core schools to start teaching children what it calls "21st Century competencies" such as "recognizing bias in sources," "flexibil-ity," "cultural awareness and competence," "appreciation for diversity," "collaboration, teamwork, cooperation," "empathy," "perspective taking, trust, service orientation," and "social influ-ence with others."[16]

There have been instances in the past when the federal govern-ment has injected itself into education, but usually with more benign purposes in mind.

In the mid-1960s, Congress first passed federal aid to ed-ucation and President Lyndon Johnson withheld funds from segregated southern schools, forcing compliance with the Supreme Court's *Brown v. Board of Education* ruling a decade earlier.

President George W. Bush passed the famous No Child Left Behind Act early in his first term. The law set up a series of tests for students in the fourth and eighth grades, and called for spe-cial attention for those students who failed and for the schools with a high failure rate. While the law influenced educational fo-cus at all levels, many complained that it forced teachers to teach to the test in an effort to maximize the number of students who passed, especially when teacher pay was linked, in some schools, to the test score improvement. Some teachers ran their classes like SAT prep courses.

As No Child Left Behind waned in popularity, forty-four states have either received waivers from the Obama administration or are currently seeking one.

But No Child Left Behind made no effort to influence how teachers taught or what subjects they covered, beyond basic reading and math. The Common Core curriculum does just that and focuses on each aspect of teaching with very specific instructions for every teacher.

While the Common Core curriculum is not required by federal law, President Obama and his Education Secretary Arne Duncan have gotten forty-four states to adopt it by dangling extra funding in their faces. They allocated about $5 billion for funds in the Race to the Top program, which rewarded the best fifteen states with the extra funds.[17]

Five billion may not seem like a lot in a $600 billion national education budget (federal plus state and local), but it was enough to get the states' attention. While only fifteen states won the "race" and got the funds, the rest fell in line with the rules of the contest, which required their adoption of the Common Core curriculum.

Rick Hess, resident Scholar and Director of Education Policy Studies at the American Enterprise Institute, describes how Common Core was adopted. "No one debated it, nobody was really aware of what it meant," Hess says. "This was unusual in that it wasn't at all debated, even though it was big and national in scope, because people were just excited about the chance of being eligible for a chunk of the money."[18]

Five states — Texas, Virginia, Nebraska, Alaska, and Minnesota — have refused to adopt Common Core. Symptomatic of how opposition is cutting across party lines, Texas, Alaska, and Nebraska are decidedly red states, while Virginia and Minnesota both went for Obama in 2008 and 2012.

Governor Rick Perry of Texas rejected the Common Core curriculum saying: "Texas is on the right path toward improved education, and we would be foolish and irresponsible to place our children's future in the hands of unelected bureaucrats and special interest groups thousands of miles away in Washington, virtually eliminating parents' participation in their children's education."[19] Indiana, which adopted the standards in 2010, has since pulled out of the program after the legislature passed and the Governor signed legislation to do so. Governor Mike Pence explained that, "Hoosiers have high expectations when it comes to Indiana schools." He added, "That's why Indiana decided to have a time-out on national education standards. When it comes to setting standards for schools, I can assure you, Indiana's will be uncommonly high. They will be written by Hoosiers, for Hoosiers, and will be among the best in the nation."[20]

At least one hundred bills have been introduced in the various state legislatures to drop out of the Common Core curriculum, and one opponent said that Indiana's action in pulling out is likely to "open the floodgates" to other states following suit.[21]

Parents, too, are spreading the word that they can choose to opt their children out of the Common Core testing protocol. A group called "iRefuse" is instructing parents that they can refuse to allow their children to be tested.

Yvonne Gasperino, one of the iRefuse rally's organizers, told Breitbart-News.com that the group's "most important goal is to create awareness for parents on how they can refuse the testing for their children."[22] Gasperino said parents are receiving misinformation, including materials sent directly from the schools about what the impact of opting out will be to the children. "It's causing some nervousness among parents," she continued. "We want to insure that all parents are equipped to refuse by providing them with websites where they can get letter templates they can use and where good, solid, factual information on refusing can be found."[23]

Beyond objections to the federal control that Common Core mandates, state education leaders balk at the one-size-fits-all character of the standards. Stephanie Bell, a member of the Alabama State Board of Education, said the standards demand that every child in the nation "be on the same page at the same time." As Bell explains, "every child is created, and I thank the Lord for this, we're all created different."[24]

Common Core Develops Massive Federal Student Database

Others object to the efforts of those who administer Common Core on the national level to gather personal data about individual students. Columnist Michelle Malkin reported that Common Core will initiate "an unprecedented nationwide student tracking system, whose data will apparently be sold by government officials to the highest bidders."[25] Malkin predicted that Common Core would amass voluminous data on each child including "health-care histories, income information, religious affiliations, voting status and even blood types and homework completion."[26]

But some warn that the Department of Education's data collection efforts go far beyond even these questionable parameters. Joy Pullmann, managing editor of *School Reform News* writes that "the feds want to use schools to catalogue 'attributes, dispositions, social skills, attitudes, and interpersonal resources — independent of intellectual ability' according to a February 2014 Department of Education report, all under the guise of education."[27]

She noted that, "the Department's report suggests researching how to measure and monitor these student attributes using 'data mining' techniques and even functional magnetic resonance imaging." Pullman adds that the Department explores "experiments on how kids respond to computer tutors, using cameras to judge facial expressions, an electronic seat that judges posture, a pressure-sensitive computer mouse and a biometric wrap on kids' wrists."[28]

The Department of Education, as part of the Common Core curriculum is "funding and mandating databases that could expand to include 'health care history, disciplinary record, family income range, family voting status and religious affiliation,' according to a 2012 report by the Pioneer Institute and the National Center for Educational Statistics. Under agreements every state signed to get 2009 stimulus funds, they must share students' academic data with the federal government."[29]

Isn't data collection as intrusive as this banned by federal privacy laws?

Not really.

Pullmann explains that "under the DOE's 2011 reinterpretation of the Federal Education Rights and Privacy Act, any local, state, or federal agency may designate any individual or organization as an 'educational representative' who can access such data as long as the agency says this access is necessary to study or evaluate a program. These can include school volunteers and private companies!" Pullman summarizes: "In short, the government wants to collect a dossier on every child, containing highly personal information without asking permission or even notifying parents."[30]

Michelle Malkin raised the specter that this intimate information "will be available to a wide variety of public agencies" and that the "Obama administration is paving the way for private entities to buy their way into the data."[31] Nine states — Colorado, Delaware, Georgia, Illinois, Kentucky, Louisiana, New York, North Carolina, and Massachusetts — originally committed to enter data into the system.

iBloom, the primary data entry system, was a joint project of the liberal Bill & Melinda Gates Foundation (which also funded the development of Common Core) and Rupert Murdoch's News Corp, which built the database infrastructure. The plan was that iBloom would collect the student data "to be stored in a data cloud that would hold incredibly detailed data points on millions of school children with the stated mission of allowing education officials to use the information to target educational support."[32] Eventually, parents and educators raised enough opposition focusing on the privacy issues surrounding the student spying project that states like New York backed down. iBloom was forced to close down in April 2014.

R.I.P.

The $100 million spent by the Gates Foundation for iBloom went down the drain. Not surprisingly, iBloom blamed its failure on "this misdirected criticism" of its outrageous plan instead of on the inappropriateness of the project in the first place.[33]

Dumbing Down Colleges

While Common Core only applies to K-12 education, it is specifically designed to bleed over into higher education, too. Because Common Core is dumbed down, ultimately SAT tests and college standards will have the same fate. Indeed, the Department of Education regulations that accompany Common Core specifically prohibit public universities and colleges in states that have accepted the curriculum from requiring remedial education for those who show up at the college door without the necessary reading or math skills for admission. Instead, they must immediately be enrolled in college credit courses. In other words, they must take the high school diploma of its newly admitted students at face value and not question their competence.

The Federal Register of April 9, 2010, Vol. 75, No. 68, pages 18, 172–18, 185 demands that states adopt "policies that exempt from remedial courses and place into credit-bearing college courses students who meet the consortium-adopted achievement standard (as defined in this notice) for those assessments . . ." That means that once you graduate from high school, you are in — no questions asked.

The experience of the City University of New York (CUNY) shows how destructive this requirement really can be. Historically,

New York City's University — especially its leading colleges (City College, Hunter, Brooklyn College, Queens College and Baruch) have enjoyed an excellent reputation. Among its alumni are nine Nobel Prize winners, former Supreme Court justice Felix Frankfurter, former secretary of state Colin Powell, and noted presidential advisor Bernard M. Baruch. (Dick's father graduated from City College, class of 1934!)

But the radicals of the '60s demanded "open admissions" — a policy where every high school graduate in New York City could be automatically admitted to any of the CUNY schools if he or she so desired. The results were catastrophic. Standards plunged and the CUNY diploma was increasingly not worth the paper on which it was written.

In 1999, CUNY ended open admissions and former Congressman Herman Badillo, himself a City College graduate, was appointed Chairman of the Board of Trustees. Badillo implemented dramatic reforms that were backed by the political clout of then Governor of New York State, George Pataki, and Mayor of New York City, Rudy Giuliani.

Badillo modified the open admissions process. High school graduates were welcome to come to CUNY, but if they failed competency tests in reading and math, they could not matriculate and take college credit courses until they passed these tests. In the meantime, they could take free, non-credit remedial courses to help them make the grade.

For some, experiences like this seem to support higher academic standards and to militate against compromising them to let more minority students in. But, to Obama and the Common Core advocates, it is a signal to dumb down colleges and the tests it takes to get into them so more people can graduate and go on to college. Remedial courses become what Dr. Peter Wood, president of the National Association of Scholars called the "on-ramp" to help students raise their performance to the grade required in college.[34]

Dr. Wood points out that, "some 1.7 million [college] freshman each year are remanded to remedial courses — 20 percent of students entering four-year universities, and more than 50 percent of those entering two-year colleges. For example, 44 percent of freshmen enrolled in the California State University system have to take either remedial English or math."[35] Wood writes that "remediation is part of the price higher education pays for its determination to open access to a college education as widely as possible."[36] Common Core does away with the "on ramp" and throws students right onto the crowded highway of higher education. At first, they watch the other cars speed by. But, in time, as the number of slower cars (students) increases, the overall speed on the highway decreases and educational standards fall.

Dumbing Down the SAT Tests

To accommodate the lower college standards made inevitable by Common Core's ban on remedial courses, the College Board is obliging by dumbing down the SAT, long used to gauge the ability to do college work. Indeed, many schools are no longer requiring the SAT at all, preferring instead to take the high school grades at face value. One reason for that may be that the so-called "architect" of the Common Core, David Coleman, became Chairman of the College Board last year. Look for some more big changes.

National Review Editor Rich Lowry explains that "the college board is updating its iconic test yet again in ways that are indistinguishable from dumbing it down. The old vocabulary words are out. The math is easier. Guessing is no longer punished in the scoring and we're made to believe that the test is better than ever."[37] Lowry recalls that ten years ago, the analogy portion of the test was scrapped and replaced by an essay. Peter Wood describes the change as beginning "of a decade long experiment in awarding points for sloppy writing graded by mindless formulae."[38]

Obama's power grab of K-12 classroom curriculum in order to dumb down our education standards is a national disgrace and a disservice to America's children. And so is his misguided decision to push kids through college without the remedial work they need. It's shameless pandering to his constituents that won't do them any good. Those are the stakes in the 2016 election. Will we insist on excellence in education or make mediocrity the new norm?

The EPA Tries to Change Every Aspect of Our Lives . . . In The Name of Climate Change

THE ULTIMATE POWER GRAB is the effort by Obama and the Environmental Protection Agency (EPA) zealots to change every aspect of our lives. It's much worse than you think: The EPA bureaucracy wants to tell us where to live and how to live, all in the name of preventing global climate change.

Citing the ultimate imperative — to keep the Earth habitable — the EPA seeks total control over our lives. Here's what they think:

- We should all live in cities, densely packed together so we only rarely have to drive (because driving emits greenhouse gases).

- We should all pay much higher prices for the cars we drive to compensate for higher mileage standards and, if possible, switch to electric cars for now and hydrogen cars in the future.

- We must stop using electricity generated by inexpensive and domestically plentiful coal and, instead, use power only from renewable sources — like solar and wind — even though they cost much more.

- We can use our increasingly huge supply of natural gas to produce power, but only as a "bridge fuel" to be used while we are developing renewable sources.

Manufacturing must adopt radical new technology to avoid carbon emissions, and the trend toward automation must abate because machines run on electricity. If that means that other nations take away our jobs, so be it.

We must monitor our electricity use in our homes and pay penalties for peak-time power.

We must buy ever more expensive appliances that use less power.

The reason for these restrictions is simple: Global climate change is coming! In fact, it's here!

To stop Obama and the EPA from controlling every aspect of our daily lives, we must defeat the Democratic Party in 2014 and 2016. By electing a Republican president, we can stop the Democrats from regulating our entire economy.

The EPA was founded on December 2, 1970, to protect us from air and water pollution. Its legislative mandate springs from the Clean Air and Clean Water Acts passed in the early years of the decade. And it has done a great job! Air and water pollution are vastly reduced in all areas of the country.

But the agency has found new life in its current mission to stop climate change. Unfortunately, Congress never gave the EPA permission to switch its purpose and it is still relying on powers granted in the original laws passed in the early 1970s to fulfill its new goal.

Pollution and global climate change are very different things. Pollution — particulate emissions, sulfur dioxide, lead, nitrous oxides primarily — make you sick and can kill. But we breathe the carbon dioxide that is said to cause climate change every minute of every day. Plants live on carbon dioxide. There is no proven health issue caused there. But, nevertheless, the EPA interprets statutes designed to stop the emission of pollution and poison into the air and water to stop the carbon release that they insist causes climate change.

So without any new laws to authorize it, or any form of congressional assent, the EPA is trying to reshape our entire economy according to its far-reaching plans.

It's not only that there's no statutory basis for the EPA power grab, but the scientific foundation on which its rationale is based is crumbling before our eyes. Scientists warn of future climate change, but reluctantly admit that not much has happened in the past two decades as a "pause in warming has set in", confounding their climate models.

In 2009, former Vice President Al Gore warned that "there is a 75 percent chance that the entire north polar ice cap, during some of the summer months, could be completely ice-free within the next five to seven years."[1] But instead of the ice cap melting, the media reported that "a chilly Arctic summer [in 2013] has left 533,000 more square miles of ocean covered with ice than at the same time last year — an increase of 29 percent."[2] What seemed like a prescient warning turned out to be a false alarm.

Models that predicted a geometric increase in warming turned out to be inaccurate. True, the Earth is getting warmer, but not by much. In the past thirty-three years, global temperatures, according to NASA, have risen by .7 degrees Fahrenheit.[3]

Scientists are very imprecise in their estimates of future global warming, all the more because they almost all failed to predict the seventeen-year pause in which we now find ourselves. The Intergovernmental Panel on Climate Change (IPCC), which includes 1,300 scientists from all over the world, forecasts a temperature rise of from 2.5 to 10 degrees Fahrenheit by 2100.[4]

Some range. At 2.5 degrees, the predicted rise in sea levels would be manageable. At 10 degrees, much less so.

The entire fabric of climate change warnings is based on projections, often unconfirmed by actual experience. The journal *Nature Climate Change* examined 117 predictions of climate change that were made in the 1990s to determine how many came true. Only three turned out to be accurate. The other 114 predicted an average of twice as much global temperature change as actually happened.[5] With the scientific data so imprecise, Congress has refused to act.

Part of the problem is political: While the US works to cut back carbon emissions, two of the biggest polluters on the planet — China and India — are unwilling to cap their carbon emissions. Along with much of the developing world, they claim that they need to emit carbons in order to catch up with the industrialization of the developed world. But even climate scientists concede that it doesn't matter which country emits carbon, the effect on climate is the same.

Faced with Chinese and Indian inaction, the Senate refused to ratify the Kyoto Accords, the global set of climate goals signed by President Clinton. The margin? 95–0!

When Obama swept into power in 2008, many environmentalists assumed that congressional action on climate change would be swift. The president proposed a complex system of Cap and Trade, which permitted power plants and manufacturers to buy and sell the right to emit carbon like the Papal indulgences of olden times.

But even with sixty compliant democratic votes in the Senate, Obama found he could not pass Cap and Trade. Senators from coal states could not see why they had to condemn their constituents to perpetual unemployment by putting their main industry out of business. And senators from all over the country — and both parties — questioned why the United States should give its principal competitor, China, a leg up by hobbling our manufacturing sector with costs and environmental burdens while Chinese industries went blithely along emitting whatever they wanted into the Earth's atmosphere. (In 2012, China emitted 27 percent of the world's greenhouse gases — more than the United States and the European Union combined.)[6]

So, having struck out before Congress, Obama turned right around and instructed his EPA to go ahead and implement the very programs by administrative fiat that had failed before the Senate and the House. Congress be damned!

John Podesta told the press exactly what the Obama administration thought about the balance of power and the president's implementation of these very programs despite Congress. Talking to reporters, Podesta pompously announced that "congress could not derail the Obama administration's efforts to unilaterally enact policies to fight global warming."[7]

Podesta admitted that Obama "was committed to using executive orders to pass regulations under the Clean Air Act to limit carbon dioxide emissions that they say cause global warming."[8]

This will be no secret power grab. Obama plans to be front and center, taunting Congress as he breaks the law in plain sight.

The legal underpinning for EPA's power grab is shaky, at best. Again, it relies on the Clean Air Act. The Supreme Court has yet to rule on the legality of the EPA power grab. In another decision, the Court held that EPA could use the Clean Air Act to regulate emissions from cars and trucks, but it said nothing about power plants and manufacturing industries.[9] No matter, EPA went ahead with its rule making anyway. The EPA's goal was not merely to cut emissions of greenhouse gases, but to revise and redesign the nation's entire electric power generation system, its manufacturing base, and its automotive industry. EPA would use global warming as an excuse to regulate not only the entire economy, but our entire lives as well.

The first step was to put coal out of business. E-mails, uncovered as a result of a Freedom of Information Act request by the conservative, legal watchdog group Judicial Watch, show an active conspiracy between the EPA and radical environmental groups to destroy the coal industry.

FOX News reported that "John Coequyt, head of Sierra's "beyond coal" campaign, wrote to [Michael] Goo [Associate Administrator for Policy at EPA] and another EPA staffer in an apparent attempt to pressure EPA into adopting regulations so strict that coal plants that already received construction permits could not be built."[10]

The e-mail from Coequyt reads: "Attached is a list of plants that the companies shelved because of uncertainty around GHG regulations. If a standard is set that these plants could meet, there is a not small chance that they (sic) company could decide to revive the proposal."[11]

The rule-makers at EPA have been busy issuing seventy-six new regulations aimed at forcing utilities to limit carbon emissions regardless of the impact on the national economy. But even as the EPA polished regulations to limit greenhouse gas emissions from power plants, the private sector cut them anyway — not because of rules or regulations, but because of market economics.

With fracking (where high pressure water is used to break up shale deposits to release gas and oil deep below the surface), US supplies of natural gas have skyrocketed, sending the price plummeting. Power plants can produce electricity for half the price, using gas instead of coal, so every day more plants are converting.

In the past decade, power from coal has dropped from 50 percent of our national output to 37 percent, while gas-generated electricity has risen from 18 percent to 29 percent.[12] (Gas emits half the carbon that coal does.) But that's not good enough for the EPA. Calling natural gas a temporary "bridge fuel," they are imposing new regulations to force businesses to switch to renewable sources. But these forms of energy — solar, wind, geothermal

— are much more expensive than either coal or gas, and forcing their adoption will send power bills through the roof. This will make our manufacturers much less competitive and send jobs packing overseas.

With 620 coal-fired plants in China,[13] Beijing is ready and willing to replace our manufacturing industries with their own.

But the coal industry has worked hard to clean up its act. "Emissions of the six principal air pollutants dropped by 67 percent."[14]

But the real advance would be to discover a mechanism to capture carbon as it comes out of a smokestack and bury it in the ground so it never enters the atmosphere.

The technology exists, but EPA won't give the coal industry the time to make it work. Meanwhile Obama says he supports these efforts and predicts that clean coal technology is "something that can make America energy independent."[15] But his EPA hasn't gotten the message. The problem is that the EPA won't wait for the science to catch up. At the end of 2013, it demanded that new coal plants immediately install carbon capture technologies as a precondition of their construction.

A spokesman for the coal industry complains that "since only the expensive first-generation technology is now available to utility companies, the EPA is making new coal plants so expensive that no utility will build one."[16] So, despite Obama's commitment that he would back clean coal technology, he is, in fact, sabotaging it.

What's the hurry? To stop global warming that isn't happening? To be sure China gets to emit carbon before we can?

The EPA's goal of regulation of all carbon emissions will reach broadly into every aspect of our lives. Not only would manufacturing and electricity-generation plants have to comply, but also so would schools and hospitals. And, of course, cars and trucks, too, will be subject to the EPA regulations. In the past, Congress has approved ever-increasing mileage standards for motor vehicles. But Obama didn't see the need to consult Congress and has imposed them on his own.

On February 18, 2012, the media reported that the Obama will "again bypass Congress and take executive actions to promote his agenda . . . this time by ordering the federal government to develop the next round of greenhouse gas standards for medium- and heavy-weight trucks by March 2016."[17] Podesta has told us it's about to happen — a massive power grab in defiance of Congress.

John Kerry's Climate Treaty: The Ultimate Bypass of Congress

And, just in case the regulatory strategy for carbon regulation doesn't work, Secretary of State John Kerry has made the negotiation and signing of a climate change treaty a top priority for 2014. *The New York Times* reported, on January 2, 2014, that Mr. Kerry has "initiated a systematic, top-down push to create an agency-wide focus on global warming. His goal is to become the lead broker of a global climate treaty in 2015 that will commit the United States and other nations to historic reductions in fossil fuel pollution."[18]

Former Senator John Kerry certainly knows that he cannot even come close to getting the sixty-seven votes required in the Senate to ratify any treaty he negotiates and signs. Indeed, he would be hard pressed to get even the sixty votes needed to bring it up for consideration. But that's not Kerry's objective. Under the Vienna Convention on the Law of Treaties, signed on May 22, 1969, any nation that signs a treaty is bound not to act contrary to its purposes even before it is ratified by the Senate.

Here's the provision:

Article 18: Obligation not to defeat the object and purpose of a treaty prior to its entry into force, a State is obliged to refrain from acts which would defeat the object and purpose of a treaty when:

a. it has signed the treaty or has exchanged instruments constituting the treaty subject to ratification, acceptance or approval, until it shall have made its intention clear not to become a party to the treaty; or

b. it has expressed its consent to be bound by the treaty, pending the entry in-to force of the treaty and provided that such entry into force is not unduly delayed.[19]

In other words, under the Vienna Convention, if Kerry signs a global climate change treaty, as a legitimate agent of the US government, we are obliged not to do anything "which would defeat the object and purpose of the treaty" even before the treaty is ratified by the Senate.

Indeed, if the Democrats hold onto control of the Senate, they will likely refuse to bring the treaty up for a vote, assuring that it remains in the limbo status of signed-but-not-yet-either-ratified-or-rejected. In limbo, the treaty has the full force of law and could be enforced by US Courts. Conceivably, it would be illegal to allow coal-fired plants to be built since their carbon emissions would defeat the purposes of the treaty. All without a word from Congress.

Only if the Republicans take control of the Senate in the elections of 2014 will they be able to defeat Kerry's transparent purposes. Upon taking control, they would presumably bring the treaty up for ratification and see it fails, ending our obligations under it imposed by the Vienna Treaty.

Kerry's attempt — doubtless with Obama's approval — is an effort to circumvent congressional approval by way of a treaty that may never be ratified or rejected.

One more power grab.

EPA Seeks to Regulate Streams and Brooks

The EPA is also trying to extend the reach of the Clean Water Act, passed in 1972, to regulate streams, brooks, and small ponds — even those on private property.

The Clean Water Act is one of the most successful pieces of legislation in modern history. Passed at the height of the environmental movement of the early 1970's — during the Nixon administration — it has cleaned up the nation's rivers, lakes, and seasides admirably, although at great cost. But, as with the equally successful Clean Air Act, the EPA is now trying to bend and shape its provisions to do something that the framers never intended: to regulate small bodies of water on private property.

Insisting that regulating smaller bodies of water is necessary to prevent larger rivers and lakes downstream from pollution, the EPA is charging ahead. Republicans have criticized the effort and questioned the science behind the proposed regulations. Science, Space, and Technology Committee Chairman Lamar Smith (R-TX) says:

> The EPA's draft water rule is a massive power grab of private property across the U.S. This could be the largest expansion of EPA regulatory authority ever. If the draft rule is approved, it would allow the EPA to regulate virtually every body of water in the United States, including private and public lakes, ponds and streams.[20]

Smith noted that "the agency's own Scientific Advisory Board (SAB) has not yet reviewed the study or EPA's draft rule to ensure that the science is sound and the data backs up the EPA's claims. But rather than allow time for independent review with input from Congress and the public, the EPA is rushing forward with a proposed rule that is based on the unverified results of the study. This rushed rule making is a clear attempt to use the study to rubber stamp the Obama administration's predetermined regulatory agenda."[21]

Smith called for the EPA to "slow down, and allow a full and fair review of the study in context by the public and independent scientists."[22] He and other Republicans worry that the proposed rule could give the EPA authority over any stream or ditch. "The government might soon be able to declare jurisdiction over a seasonal stream in your backyard."[23] Republicans also worry that it might make it harder to expand building space on your property or to sell your land to private developers. Indeed, some suspect that these side effects might be the very purpose of the EPA rule making.

The Supreme Court ruled that the expansion of the EPA rules was legal as long as the agency could demonstrate "a significant nexus" between the new bodies of water to be regulated and those currently under EPA jurisdiction.[24]

Unlike with greenhouse gases, the EPA denies that the proposed new rule is a big deal. Jan Goldman-Carter, senior wetlands and water resources counsel with the National Wildlife Fund and a supporter of the new rule, says the EPA is just establishing "with scientific criteria, the kind of wetlands and water bodies that have a 'significant nexus' to protected waters."[25]

She insists the new rule is "almost entirely about clarification. The big difference is it will all be understood up front so you won't have to waste agencies' time and resources and landowners' time and resources doing it all case-by-case."[26]

But those used to the ways of the EPA point out that the changes under the new rule are likely to be enormous. FOX News reports that the law firm of Bracewell & Giuliani, LLP, predicts that the proposed rule "could have significant impact on infrastructure, energy and land development."[27] They warn that under the new rule, "definitions would be changed in more than one way, with 'perhaps the most significant' being that many waters and wetlands would meet the 'significant nexus' label automatically, bypassing the 'fact intensive inquiry' they might have gone through to get those protections in the past."[28]

Critics of the new rule, such as Congressman Smith, say that the EPA is basing its analysis of the nation's streams and brooks on a draft environmental report that has yet to be fully vetted by the Independent Science Advisory Board. State and local officials, in particular, are up in arms over the proposed expansion of federal jurisdiction. Nita Taylor, county manager of Lincoln, New Mexico, told her fellow commissioners she interpreted the report as the EPA and Army Corps of Engineers seeking to "gain jurisdiction over all water in the United States, and all activities affecting all water; and to regulate water now considered entirely under state jurisdiction."[29]

David Winkles, Farm Bureau president, says that the standard of "significant nexus" is not being met in the federal study. Rather, he says that if there is any "measurable connection" between local streams or brooks and major bodies of water, EPA will use it to assert jurisdiction.[30]

As Congressman Smith notes: "The EPA's own science advisors have not had the opportunity to review the science underpinning this rule," he said. "Any rule that could give EPA the authority to tell us what to do in our own backyards needs to be supported by sound science."[31]

EPA'S Real Agenda: Global Governance

What is behind the EPA-on-steroids? Why the aggressive rule making? Is it just overzealous environmental protection? Or is there something more — much more — at work.

We suspect Agenda 21 is at play here. Agenda 21 is an ultra-left framework for global development adopted by the UN at the Rio Conference of 1992. In effect, it aims to coordinate all the world's land use, energy, transportation, zoning, residential living, business location, and environmental policies to fight climate change and to minimize the emission of greenhouse gases. Every global policy must bend toward the single goal of stopping global warming! Adopted before it became clear that climate change was far less of a danger than initially supposed, the left has not backed away from Agenda 21, but doubled down on some of its most offensive provisions.

Agenda 21 specifies how the world needs to be reorganized to fight climate change — and, by implication, grants the UN the power to do so. There needs to be great changes. Cities, for example, have to become the most popular place to live so people won't drive cars that emit carbon. Suburbs and rural areas have to go. Housing density must increase. Tiny micro apartments, of the sort promoted by former New York City Mayor Michael Bloomberg, are the way of the future. Mass transit must replace the car and we must learn to live in a world without automobiles.

The EPA espouses many of the goals of Agenda 21. In Denver, for example, a project called "Living Streets," pushed by the EPA, actually advocates increasing traffic and congestion by reducing and merging lanes in high traffic areas as a first step to get people to drive less — with no regard for either the economic impact on businesses or the personal toll on drivers. *Denver Post* writer Vincent Carroll describes the program and concludes that it's really about "restricting mobility."[32]

Behind Agenda 21 lies not just a fear of climate change, but a desire for global governance on every level. The stakes go far beyond greenhouse emissions. They concern the very concept of American sovereignty.

The effort to move toward global governance has its intellectual and financial roots in the Club of Rome, an organization whose members were among the world's most influential people, including David Rockefeller, Jimmy Carter, Al Gore, Mikhail Gorbachev, and a host of other former foreign leaders, including the ex-presidents of Brazil, Mexico, and Canada, and the King of Spain.

According to its website, The Club — the epicenter of the push for globalism — was founded in 1968 when "a small international group of professionals from the fields of diplomacy, industry, academia, and civil society met at a quiet villa in Rome." Invited by Italian industrialist Aurelio Peccei and Scottish scientist Alexander King, they came together to discuss the dilemma of prevailing short-term thinking in international affairs and, in particular, the concerns regarding unlimited resource consumption in an increasingly interdependent world."[33]

Their first major publication, the *Limits of Growth*, was published in 1972 with stern warnings about the coming fiasco of global overpopulation. When that turned out not to be so, they shifted their push away from controlling the slow-growing world population to the area of climate change.

In the Club's book, *The First Global Revolution* by King and Bernard Schneider (Hyderabad; Orient Longman, 1993), the globalists lay out the correlation between the climate change issue and their ambitions to subordinate national sovereignty to global governance. Addressing the need to induce people to give up their attachment to nation-states, they write of the need for a "common adversary . . . to bring the divided nations together to face an outside enemy."[34]

The enemy can be "either a real one or else one invented for the purpose."[35]

The language of the book is chilling. The idea of inventing an "outside enemy" to serve as a pretext for overcoming national sovereignty is frightening. But this is not some ranting of a conspiracy theorist on the right. It is a quote from the official publication of the Club of Rome, which has influenced global policy making for three decades.

At first, the globalists hoped that the threat of overpopulation would be the "outside enemy" against which the world should unite. But, when it became evident that population drops as countries develop and that global population will start to shrink after 2050, they needed a new theme. And, Eureka! the globalists who wrote the *First Global Revolution* found it in global warming. They actually write in their book: "In searching for a new enemy to unite us, we came up with the idea that pollution, the threat of global warming, water shortages, famine, and the like could fill the bill . . . The real enemy then, is humanity itself."[36]

But Climate Change Is Only a Means to an End: Global Governance Is the Goal

Austrian philosopher Friedrich Hayek explained, in his seminal work, *The Road to Serfdom*, how freedom can be lost if one major goal (like climate change) is erected over all others. When "single minded idealists greatly exaggerate the importance of the ends they place foremost," the impetus toward central planning and the consequent erosion of freedom becomes irresistible.[37] By focusing on the claimed cataclysmic results of climate change and using the imperative of averting it, these "idealists" can shape the world to their specifications, overriding democracy — the voice of the people — and the freedom to live and work as we choose.

This is the real motive behind the massive EPA expansion of power and the efforts of Obama to extend its reach into every facet of our lives. Today, the agency is yelling about climate change. Tomorrow, it will be about the size and location of our houses. The EPA needs to be stopped.

With the evidence of at least a slowing of global warming, if not an outright reversal, why push ahead with such nation-changing regulations as the EPA is now advocating? Why, indeed, if the goal is simply to solve a problem affecting the world's climate? But the EPA's sights are not set so low. It wants to change the world itself, regardless of the climate.

And Obama is determined to accomplish this massive power grab before he either loses the democratic majority in the Senate or goes home. But when he goes home, if he first hands the baton to a Democrat, the assault on our economy and way of life will continue. That's why the 2016 election will determine the kind of country we have.

CHAPTER 4

Blocking Energy Independence

IN MEDIEVAL TIMES, NOBODY could plant or hunt on the King's land. Those who dared to enter to kill one of the King's deer and were caught usually paid with their heads.

Now, President Obama has imitated the kings of old by denying oil and gas drilling permits to all lands within his control. Dan Kish, senior vice president of the Institute for Energy Research says that although federal lands "belong to taxpayers, regulators behave as if they are the king's lands and waters, which no one dare touch."[1]

Kish notes that the federal government owns more land, by far, than private and state owners, and that "the Congressional Research Service found that 96 percent of the increased production in oil over the last five years came from those private and state lands."[2]

Kish says that thanks to Obama's policies, only the very largest companies can "survive the bureaucratic and legal hassles of operating on federal lands."[3]

President Obama's energy program is one great hypocrisy: While he celebrates America's growing energy independence, he does everything in his power — and more — to stop it and to prolong our dependence on foreign oil.

Obama and his EPA and Interior Departments have grabbed as much power as they possibly can to thwart, retard, delay, and hobble efforts to enhance domestic energy production.

Yet, this has not stopped him from boasting that he has brought America closer to energy independence than it has ever been. Whitehouse.gov reports, jubilantly, that "since President Obama took office, America's dependence on foreign oil has decreased every year. During his first term, net imports of foreign oil and petroleum fell to their lowest level in nearly twenty years. We are now less reliant on oil imports than any time since 1993."[4]

The website also brags that: "Domestic oil and natural gas production has increased every year President Obama has been in office. In 2012, domestic oil production climbed to the highest level in fifteen years and natural gas production reached an all-time high."[5] But what the website fails to note is that the very policies that have achieved these milestones have been opposed by the Obama administration with every fiber of its being. Far from encouraging domestic energy production, it has done all it can to block it, increasing regulation, raising fees, and denying drilling permits in record numbers. And where he didn't have the power to cripple our bid for energy independence, he grabbed for more.

It's not that Obama wants us to depend on foreign oil. It's just that he couldn't care less. His priority is to reduce greenhouse gas emissions by switching from oil, coal, or gas to wind, solar, and geothermal energy.

He doesn't care where the coal, oil, and gas come from — here or abroad — he just wants less of it. The fact that his dream of renewable sources remains a distant vision on the far-away horizon seems not to matter at all. He wants to force us in that direction all to mitigate greenhouse emissions.

So the increase in US oil and gas production has come about despite Obama's regulatory efforts to the contrary.

Obama has restricted drilling on federal lands, using every trick in the book to do so. He has invented regulations where none existed and appropriated to himself power no other president has used — all to stop drilling on federal or federally regulated land. As a result, while oil and gas production on federal land has dropped by 6 percent since Obama took office, it has soared on privately-owned and state-owned land (which lies beyond even this president's regulator power). In the last ten years, fossil fuel production on these non-federal lands has increased by 27 percent.[6] Meanwhile, the number of federal drilling permits issued for lands owned by Washington has dropped by 36 percent over the same period.[7] The average wait for approval of a federal drilling permit is now 307 days compared with a mere ten days in North Dakota, where the bulk of the Bakken shale formation — so productive of gas and oil — is located.[8]

Due to the boom in state- and private-land drilling, the US oil production is expected to climb from 6.5 million barrels per day in 2008 to 8.5 million in 2014.[9] While we imported 60 percent of our oil in 2005, we now import only 40 percent.[10]

The result is, as Kish says, that thanks to Obama's policies, only the very largest companies can "survive the bureaucratic and legal hassles of operating on federal lands."[11] The Obama administration's slow-walking of drilling permits flies in the face of Washington's voracious need for more revenue. Due to federal cancellations and regulatory hurdles, royalties and rentals on federal lands — money that goes to the taxpayer — are down by $12 billion since Obama took office. A recent Louisiana State University and Wharton School study estimated that simply allowing access to federal lands for drilling would create between 552,000 and 2 million new jobs by 2050 and would generate $2.7 trillion in additional revenue over that same time period.[12]

But we cannot expand our offshore oil production as long as the administration keeps its foot on the brake. With 87 percent of the off-shore area in federal hands,[13] Obama is striving to kill off the very increase in production he heralds in his speeches.

Obama was adamant in his debate with Governor Mitt Romney in the 2012 presidential race that he was not stopping oil and gas production:

Romney: "In the last four years, you cut permits and licenses on federal land and federal waters in half."

Obama: "Not true, Governor Romney."

Romney: "So how much did you cut them by?"

Obama: "It's not true."

Romney: "And — and — and production on private — on government lands is down."

Obama: "And the production is up. No it isn't."

Romney: "Production on government land of oil is down 14 percent."

Obama: "Governor —"

Romney: "And production of gas is down 9 percent."

Obama: "What you're saying is just not true. It's just not true."[14]

Factcheck.org, an arm of the Annenberg Center for Public Policy says that the "facts, for the most part, were on Romney's side,"[15] in their October 16, 2012, debate exchange.

The Center reported that:

1. "Obama was wrong when he denied Romney's claim that the Obama administration cut in half the number of new permits and new leases for offshore oil and gas drilling. The decrease is actually more than half.

2. Romney exaggerated, however, when he said the number of new permits and new leases for onshore drilling also declined by half under Obama. The decline isn't that steep.

3. Obama was wrong when he told Romney it's "just not true" that domestic oil production on federal lands is down 14 percent and gas production has fallen 9 percent in one year. Production of oil and natural gas on federal lands and in federal waters did indeed fall by those percentages as Romney said, although Romney erred in saying the drops took place "this year." The decreases occurred in fiscal year 2011."[16]

When Congress wouldn't act to keep lands off-limits for energy drilling, Obama just went around it to ban virtually all oil production in nearly half of the 23.5 million acre National Petroleum Reserve in Alaska. The Reserve was designated by Congress in 1976 as a strategic oil and natural gas stockpile to meet the energy needs of the nation.[17]

Now, by executive fiat, Obama has restricted access to almost half of the preserve, blocking drilling for up to 15 billion barrels of oil.[18] (The National Petroleum Reserve is distinct from the Arctic National Wildlife Reserve — ANWR — which has become a political *cause celebre* on the left, and is still off-limits for energy drilling.)

About 1.5 million acres of the National Petroleum Reserve is environmentally sensitive, but that area has already been carved out by previous executive action and is protected from drilling. *The Wall Street Journal* reports that "most of the other 11.5

million acres are almost indistinguishable from acreage owned by the state that is being drilled safely nearby."[19]

Both of Alaska's Senators, Democrat Mark Begich and Republican Lisa Murkowski, wrote to Interior Secretary Ken Salazar protesting against what they called "the largest wholesale land withdrawal and blocking of access to an energy resource by the federal government in decades."[20] This decision, they add, "will cause serious harm to the economy and energy security of the United States, as well as to the state of Alaska."[21] Mr. Begich is a Democrat.

In each of its budgets, the administration has sought to raise taxes on the oil and gas industry, pursuant to its agenda of tipping the playing field to advantage renewable sources no matter how uneconomical.

From its very first days in office, the Obama administration has taken step after step to limit, ban, or reduce the scope of drilling for energy throughout the nation:

- **Feb. 4, 2009** — Withdrew seventy-seven oil and gas leases in Utah

- **Feb. 10, 2009** — Delayed five-year program of offshore oil leasing

- **July 20, 2009** — Blocked uranium mining in Arizona

- **Oct. 20, 2009** — Announced new rules on offshore drilling leases; the result was an 85 percent drop in oil industry interest in bidding

- **Jan. 26, 2010** — Delayed offshore leasing in Virginia

- **March 12, 2010** — Withdrew sixty-one oil leases in Montana

- **March 31, 2010** — Closed large portions of our offshore areas to drilling

- **May 6, 2010** — Issued a moratorium on new oil and gas leases in the Gulf

- **May 17, 2010** — Announced new hurdles to onshore oil and gas drilling

- **Nov. 18, 2010** — Postponed all Gulf leases until 2012

- **Dec. 1, 2010** — Banned new leasing in Gulf Coast, East and West Coasts, and parts of Alaska, stopping new production until 2017

- **Dec. 23, 2010** — Issued a new "Wild Lands" executive order, placing hundreds of millions of acres off-limits for energy production

- **Feb. 2, 2011** — Federal judge finds administration in contempt for slow-walking drilling permits in the Gulf

- **Jan. 9, 2013** — Bans uranium mining on one million acres of federal land for twenty years

- **Jan. 12, 3013** — Imposed Ocean Zoning plan, which put huge parts of the Gulf off-limits for US drilling

- **Feb. 3, 2013** — Banned fracking on federal land in Utah, Wyoming, and Colorado[22]

Some of these regulatory decisions lay within the power of the executive and are protected by precedent. But others were simply power grabs to stop energy development where Obama could do so.

The most egregious limitation on the oil and gas industries imposed by Obama has been its refusal to permit the Keystone Pipeline to proceed. Even if the pipeline ultimately gets federal approval, the five-year delay in doing so has already inflicted irreparable harm on our economy.

Keystone is designed to carry synthetic crude oil from the Alberta Sands in Canada to refineries in Texas and Louisiana.

The pipeline's first three segments have been approved — the third one only on March 22, 2012. But the fourth part — which will extend from Hardisty, Alberta, to Steele City, Nebraska — is still under government review.

In January, 2012, Obama rejected the fourth phase and the TransCanada Corporation, the pipeline's sponsor, changed its route to minimize "the disturbance of land, water resources, and special areas."[23] But despite the change, the fourth phase is still hanging fire. In fact, the dangers of the pipeline have little to do with the real issues blocking its approval. The US has over 2 million miles of pipeline currently carrying oil with few if any mishaps and no environmental damage.[24] The State Department has already conducted three studies, all of which prove that the pipeline would do no harm to the environment.

The real reason environmentalists have persuaded Obama to withhold his approval is that they seek to minimize oil production in the Alberta tar sands. They maintain that extraction by this method increases the amount of methane gas released into the atmosphere by 9 percent over conventional oil drilling,[25] worsening global warming.

Of course, if Canada cannot sell the oil to the United States, China stands ready and willing to take it on without regard for any supposed environmental damage. Canada threatens to build a pipeline across its territory from Alberta to Winnipeg from which the oil could be shipped to Chinese ports.

Hanging in the balance are at least 20,000 "shovel-ready" jobs and the ability to carry up to one million barrels of oil per day.[26]

But the danger of environmental damage has very little to do with Obama's anti-oil policy. His administration slow-walks approval of Gulf drilling permits, tries to kill the Keystone Pipeline, and attempts to minimize drilling on federal lands for the same reason: The officials want to replace oil and gas with renewable energy sources.

Driven by their fear of global climate change, they want to make oil and gas more costly so that solar, wind, geothermal, biofuels, and other renewable strategies can gain traction.

But, apart from hydroelectric power, which has been around for ages, renewables still account for only a tiny proportion of American energy. Combined, all of the other technologies provide only 7 percent of the energy in the nation. When Obama took office, they accounted for 2 percent. The expansion has been rapid, but the growth still leaves coal, natural gas, and nuclear power as the major sources of electricity in the country.

But, nevertheless, Obama continues his war on oil, coal and natural gas. While he speaks of the need for energy independence and happily takes credit for any progress in that direction, he really only wants to minimize any non-renewable sources. He claims this is to stop climate change and global warming, which many believe isn't really happening anyway.

Our growing energy independence is the source of potentially growing strength. That's why Obama wants to block it. For a strong America, which does not need foreign oil, we have got to win the presidential election in 2016.

CHAPTER 5

Obama Guts Welfare Reform

ONE OF THE MOST successful federal programs in the past forty years was the ground-breaking reform of the welfare system enacted by Congress and signed into law by President Bill Clinton in 1996. For the first time in history, welfare recipients were required to work in order to receive federal benefits. The new law also set a lifetime limit of five years for any person to receive benefits. After that, they were no longer eligible under any circumstances. The success of the law is legendary. Welfare rolls dropped in half and the child poverty level dropped to its lowest in history. After the passage of the reform, 3.5 million people left poverty behind, including 2.9 million children, of whom 1.2 million were African-American. Hunger in the United States dropped by half.[1]

House Ways and Means Chairman David Camp (R-MI) hailed the program for leading "to more work, more earnings, less welfare dependence, and less poverty among families headed by low-income single mothers."[2]

But the law remained an irritant to Obama's liberal constituents who lamented the passing of the traditional welfare program, the only entitlement ever to be repealed. They wanted the work requirement gone.

And Obama was very willing to oblige them.

On July 12, 2012, the president suddenly gutted the program by enacting rules that clearly violated the letter and the spirit of the law. Not only that, but the way that Obama did it was illegal. The president absolutely did not have the authority to make such a fundamental change in a federal entitlement program by simply sending out a memo. Any change of this magnitude required an act of Congress.

It was nothing more than another big power grab by Obama. Once again, Obama did it all on his own. He never asked Congress for the authority to make revisions in the welfare work law, as he was required to do. He simply permitted HHS to issue an "Information Memorandum," which unilaterally gave states permission to waive the work rules.[3]

Under the welfare reform bill that President Clinton signed, states were required to show that 50 percent of single-headed, welfare-receiving families — and 90 percent of two-parent families — were involved in work activities. "What constitutes 'work activities' is not necessarily a job; training, job-search assistance, volunteer work, vocational and skills training, and some forms of education and childcare work are included."[4] Obama independently waived the work requirement for states, asking only that they demonstrate that a significant number of their recipients had actually left the rolls each month. But that meant nothing, since the normal turnover in cases could easily accomplish that. Turnover is no indication that people are going to work, only that they are entering the revolving door that frequently leads recipients right back to the same dependency.

Congressman Camp (R-MI) recognized the power grab. ". . . without any thought of consulting Congress, as is required by law, the administration saw fit to unilaterally waive the work requirements and risk the progress that has been made in the last 16 years."[5]

Camp criticized the Obama administration for overstepping its authority to waive the requirement, "especially through a simple guidance document from HHS."[6]

Republicans were suspicious all along that a liberal, democratic president would someday come along and dilute the welfare reform act. So, during the drafting of the reform bill, they made sure that the official account of the Act's legislative history included a statement that: "Waivers granted after the date of enactment may not override provisions of the TANF law that concern mandatory work requirements."[7]

But Obama ran right through that red light and made whatever changes he wanted anyway.

It's not just the Republicans who found this to be improper. The nonpartisan Congressional Research Service concluded that the work requirements in the 1996 reform bill could not be waived. "Effectively, there are no TANF waivers" that are permitted.[8]

The House was determined to stop Obama's unconstitutional and illegal initiative. On March 13, 2013, it voted to override Obama's waivers on work requirements, but without the concurrence of the Democratic Senate, the changes will stand unless they are overturned by a court.

One more giant power grab by Obama.

CHAPTER 6

The FCC Tries to Regulate the Internet

O NE OF THE LEAST reported and most stealth power grabs has been Obama's efforts to put the Internet under his regulatory thumb.

Ever since the Internet was invented (not by Al Gore!) governments at all levels have worked overtime to regulate it, thus far without success.

It galls dictatorships from Beijing to Moscow that they cannot control what their people read online. China, for example, employs 2 million people as Internet censors and controllers, all focused on restricting what their people are allowed to read online.

But here at home, the most serious threat to internet freedom comes from the regulatory ambitions of the Federal Communications Commission (FCC).

Originally, the FCC tried to get its nose into the tent of Internet control by promulgating the doctrine of "Net Neutrality," which sought to stop Internet Service Providers (ISPs) from charging different fees to different web users for their hosting services. The ISPs have wanted to offer special, high-speed access to web content providers who are willing to pay for it. Taking advantage of broad public opposition to the idea, the FCC tried to bar it by regulation.

Many people approve of the principle of net neutrality, but do not want the FCC to impose it since, in doing so, it would acquire the jurisdiction to regulate all aspects of the Internet.

The Internet Service Providers sued the Obama FCC to block the Net Neutrality rule and won a verdict in the DC Court of Appeals on January 14, 2014. The Court struck down the FCC regulation saying that the agency was subjecting Internet providers to the same thicket of regulation that it used to police traditional phone companies subject to its jurisdiction.

But rather than appeal the ruling, FCC Chairman Tom Wheeler — appointed by Obama — announced a new plan to regulate the Internet based on a different rationale than that which the Court had struck down. Instead, the FCC is looking to acquire power over the Internet by exploiting a provision of the Telecommunications Act passed by Congress in 1995. A well-meaning piece of non-controversial legislation, its Section 706 provides that:

- "The Commission shall encourage the deployment on a reasonable and timely basis of advanced telecommunications capability to all Americans by utilizing price cap regulation, regulatory forbearance, measures that promote competition in the local telecommunications market, or other regulating methods that remove barriers to infrastructure investment."[1]

- "It shall take immediate action to accelerate deployment of such capability by removing barriers to infrastructure investment and by promoting competition in the telecommunications market."[2]

In the hands of the power-grabbing Obama dministration, these seemingly innocuous provisions are sufficient to justify a whole range of regulations, which, taken together, imperil the freedom of the Internet.

As the hot breath of government regulation draws nearer, Google and other top Internet companies are getting "nervous."

National Journal reports that "Google's lawyers have said they're worried how the FCC may use its newfound powers."[3]

National Journal warned that "the FCC could, theoretically, order Internet service providers and search engines to block websites offering illegal copies of music and movies."[4]

Harold Feld, the senior vice president of Public Knowledge, finds the FCC overreach "very troubling."[5] Feld suggested the FCC "could impose privacy protection regulations on Google and other companies under the theory that people would be more likely to use the Internet if they felt their personal information was safe."[6] Feld also said that the order of Google's search results could also be a target for regulation.[7] Competitors like Microsoft and Yelp have long accused Google of manipulating its search results to favor its own services. *National Journal* speculated that "app stores, smart-home devices, instant messaging, and cybersecurity are just a few other possible areas for FCC regulation."[8]

Republican critics of the FCC power grab say the government rules hinder innovation in the marketplace by preventing Internet providers from experimenting with new business models.

"No matter how many times the court says 'no,' the Obama administration refuses to abandon its furious pursuit of these harmful policies to put government in charge of the web," Reps. Fred Upton (R-MI) and Greg Walden (R-OR) said in a statement, noting that "these regulations are a solution in search of a problem."[9]

The FCC's two Republican members, Mike O'Rielly and Ajit Pai, dissented strongly from Wheeler's decision. "I am deeply concerned by the announcement that the FCC will begin considering new ways to regulate the Internet,"[10] O'Rielly said in a statement.

Section 706 of the Telecommunications Act "does not provide any affirmative regulatory authority,"[11] O'Rielly said, and a power-hungry FCC could use Wheeler's interpretation of the law "not just to regulate broadband providers, but eventually edge providers,"[12] or the companies that provide Internet content, like Netflix.

FCC Commissioner Ajit Pai also criticized Wheeler for not running his proposal past Congress. "In the wake of a court defeat, an FCC Chairman floats a plan for rules regulating Internet service providers' network management practices instead of seeking guidance from Congress . . . 'I am skeptical that this effort will end any differently from the last.'"[13]

The FCC is not alone in seeking to govern, regulate, control, and curb the free Internet. Lurking in the background, eager to step in and exert control over the Net is the United Nations, pushed by its worst members: Russia and China. In December, 2012, just weeks after the 2012 US presidential election, representatives of all the world's nations convened in Dubai to consider global control of the Internet. Responding to an initiative proposed by Russia, China, Brazil, and India, but personally formulated by Russian leader Vladimir Putin, the convention weighed giving the International Telecommunications Union (ITU) control over the Net.

The ITU was established in 1865 to regulate international telegraph services and has expanded its jurisdiction to cover telephone service among nations and communications satellites. It is headed by Hamadoun Toure of Mali, who was educated at the Technical Institute of Electronics and Telecommunication of Leningrad and at the Moscow Technical University of Communications and Informatics. His schooling in the 1980s in Leonid Brezhnev's USSR made him the perfect tool for Putin's plan to regulate the Internet. ITU's deputy director is from China.

The Russian proposal was to cede to the ITU the authority to assign Internet domain names (.com and .org names), to allow countries to control the Net within their own borders, and to permit nations to charge their citizens a special fee to access extra-national websites and to allow censorship of the Internet within each country's own borders. Most threatening was the provision that would require that the actual names and addresses of the owners of each domain name be reported to their own government, making it much easier for China to track down dissenters and punish them.

Eventually, the Dubai Conference resulted in a resolution, signed by eighty-nine nations — but boycotted by the US and Europe — establishing an international UN control of the Net. Since the resolution did not have an adequate number of signatures, it is not a treaty, but it remains an alternative framework for Internet governance — one crafted and pushed by authoritarian regimes seeking to clamp down on free speech.

Civil liberties groups — like Reporters Without Borders — worry that authoritarian governments can use the power to name and catalogue domain names to stop dissident groups from accessing the Net.

In the name of preventing spam, the Resolution also says that nations may "undertake appropriate measures to protect the physical and operational security of networks, countering unsolicited electronic communication (e.g., spam); and protection of information and personal data (e.g., phishing)."[14]

Reporters Without Borders worries that "some government could use this provision as grounds for the deployment of blocking and filtering mechanisms"[15] to block free speech online. The Resolution allows Deep Packet Inspections (DPI), which would enable governments "to access the content of emails, instant messaging exchanges and VoIP conversations,"[16] posing a serious threat to "the confidentiality of online communications."[17]

But no sooner did the United Nations seek to grab power over the Internet than the obliging Obama administration hands it over. On March 14, 2014, US officials "announced plans to relinquish federal government control over the administration of the Internet."[18]

The Internet is operated by ICANN (Internet Commission on Names and Numbers), a body of technical experts operating under the loose contractual supervision of the US Department of Commerce. Rarely, if ever, does the Department tell ICANN what to do, and ICANN's techies are perfectly fine with the arrangement. ICANN oversees the assigning of Internet domains — such as .com, .edu, and .gov — and, as *The Post* reports, "ensures that the various companies and universities involved in directing digital traffic do so safely."[19]

But, suddenly, early in 2014, the Commerce Department said it would not renew ICANN's contract.

Who will inherit ICANN's power? Foreign governments? The United Nations? Benign regulators from the business and technical communities?

So, even as the Federal Communications Commission seeks to regulate the Internet at home, the Obama administration seems intent on handing overall control to some new organization of foreign governments.

Many foreign governments — including our staunchest allies — are no longer willing to allow the United States to maintain exclusive control over the Internet. Rattled by revelations of how the National Security Agency (NSA) has intruded upon the Net, conducting surveillance and invading privacy of ordinary citizens and foreign diplomats, they are demanding that the United States surrender its control over the Net.

The Washington Post reported that while "the practical consequences of the decision [to relinquish control of the Net] were not immediately clear . . . but it could alleviate rising global complaints that the United States essentially controls the Web and takes advantage of its oversight role to help spy on the rest of the world."[20]

But if ICANN is not going to assign domain names and run the Internet, who will? The Dubai Treaty, with eighty-nine signatories, is waiting in the wings to assert governance and control.

Former House Speaker Newt Gingrich reacted with alarm to the divestiture of ICANN by the Commerce Department, saying the decision "risks foreign dictatorships defining the Internet." He said "every American should worry about Obama giving up control of the Internet to an undefined group. This is very, very dangerous."[21]

Senator John Thune (R-SD), ranking Republican member on the Senate Commerce Committee, was particularly strong on this issue, saying the Internet "needs — and deserves — a strong multi-stakeholder system free from the control of any government or governmental entity."[22] He warned that "there are people who want to see the Internet fall into the grip of the United Nations or who would allow ICANN to become an unaccountable organization with the power to control the Internet, and we cannot allow them to determine how this process plays out," he said. But he added, "I trust the innovators and entrepreneurs more than the bureaucrats — whether they're in DC or Brussels."[23]

With the FCC pressing for greater US government control over the Net and the United Nations demanding more of a voice, Internet freedom is now clearly in danger. Can it navigate between the twin shoals of an acquisitive federal government seeking to regulate it and global dictators trying to suppress it?

Conclusion

When our founders met to compose our Constitution, they faced a crucial decision at the very outset of their deliberations: Whether to follow the British model — the only quasi-democratic system in the world — or to create an entirely new form of government.

They opted not to adopt the parliamentary form of government used in England and, instead, to craft a totally new species: A system of three branches, each checking and balancing the other two.

These two systems of government are very, very different.

Parliamentary government does not mean that the legislature is supreme. It really means the opposite. It is basically an elected dictatorship. The majority party in parliament chooses the prime minister and his cabinet, collectively called the government. Once it does, it is obliged to stand with them and ratify their major programs. Should they fail to do so, the government is deemed to have lost the confidence of the parliament and has to resign. Then, the majority party can either choose a new government or call for a new election to choose a new parliament and start all over. Every member of the majority party who sits in parliament is supposed to back his party all the time. Defections are rare.

But a system of checks and balances assumes that the president and Congress will often be at cross purposes. Elected separately for different terms of office, the one is supposed to check and balance the other.

The parliamentary system seeks to discern the general will in an election and then to implement it without delay.

Our system, by contrast, assumes that competing interests will have different ideas. The Constitution dictates the rules of that game.

It's fine when one of the contending forces that shape our democracy win, prevailing over the other side by making their case better to the voters. But when one side cheats, breaks the rules, and then wins, it is far less edifying. In fact, it is revolting!

The theme of this book is that Obama is breaking the rules laid down by our Constitution. He's winning by cheating.

The Constitution is explicit: "It is Congress that has the exclusive power to legislate." But Obama is using his executive authority to act without even asking our elected legislators.

The Constitution says that the president needs to ask for the "advice and consent" of the US Senate when he makes appointments. But Obama has gamed the system by restricting debate in the Senate and by appointing "czars" who don't need confirmation.

The Constitution says that the executive shall "take care that the laws are faithfully executed." But Obama has done the opposite, refusing to enforce laws with which he doesn't agree, waiving the very legislative requirements he's charged with enforcing.

The Constitution guarantees freedom of speech. But Obama has used the agencies he controls — the IRS and the Federal Election Commission — to repress people who would express opinions that differ from his.

The Constitution guarantees people, corporations, and unions the right to participate in political campaigns, but the IRS is hitting them with audits and regulations that punish them for doing so.

The Constitution promises freedom of the press. But Obama and Attorney General Eric Holder have used illegal wiretaps and equally illegal seizure of phone records to track down public officials who speak to the media and go after them for daring to speak the truth.

The Constitution leaves up to the judiciary the right to mete out sentences to those convicted of crimes. But Obama's Justice Department is taking away the power by instructing US Attorneys to request light sentences for drug dealers and freeing thousands that have already been incarcerated.

What are we to do to restore constitutional government in America? How can we stop this nation from becoming an elected dictatorship? How can we keep the delicate system of checks and balances from being gamed by a president bent on its destruction?

The only answer is to win the presidency in 2016.

Obama is bad. His programs are worse. We must win by explaining their impact to every American.

For those who work with their hands, we need to make them realize that his global warming policies will take away their jobs even as his immigration programs deluge the market with cheap labor.

We have to show our taxpayers that Obama's entitlement policies are based on a political calculation that he can rob those who earn and pay those who loaf.

Those who walk our streets must come to realize that he is letting the worst offenders out of prison and handcuffing our efforts to keep us safe.

Parents must grasp how Obama is dumbing down our schools, letting students graduate who are unprepared for the real world and ill-equipped for anything but welfare.

The elderly need to be made to see how he is weakening Medicare and basing our health care system on a rationing of services that makes them justify the treatment they get based on how many years remain to them.

The average working person needs to understand how premium increases triggered by ObamaCare, utility bill hikes caused by EPA regulations, and taxes imposed by the government eat up their paychecks and diminish their ability to afford a comfortable life.

It is only by bringing the theoretical harms home to people in actual, real-life terms that we can defeat Obama's Democrats in 2016.

This book is designed to provide ammunition for the forces who battle for change. Aim well and keep firing!

References

Introduction

1. "a swipe at the": Dave Boyle, "Obama Blames Structural Design of Founding Fathers for Gridlock," *The Washington Times*, May 23, 2014, http://www.washingtontimes.com/news/2014/may/23/ obama-blames-structural-design-congress-gridlock/.

2. twenty-two separate: Tyler Hartsfield and Grace-Marie Turner, "41 Changes to ObamaCare . . . So Far," Galen Institute, April 8, 2014, http://www.galen.org/newsletters/changes-to-obamacare-so-far/.

3. "Nowhere in the Constitution": "ACRU: White House Rewriting of ObamaCare Violates Constitutional Separation of Powers," TheACRU.gov, April 22, 2104, http://theacru.org/acru/acru_white_ house_rewriting_of_obamacare_violates_constitutional_separation _of_powers/.

4. "I'm not concerned": Sarah Kliff, "The White House Keeps Changing Omabacare. Is that Legal?" *The Washington Post*, August 7, 2013, http://www.washingtonpost.com/blogs/wonkblog/wp/2013/08/07/ the-white-house-keeps-changing-obamacare-is-that-legal/.

5. $27 million and $7 million: Podesta Group, OpenSecrets.org, http://www.opensecrets.org/lobby/firmsum.php?id=D000022193&year=2014.

6. "could not derail": Michael Bastash, "Podesta: Congress Can't Stop Obama on Global Warming," *The Daily Caller*, May 5, 2014, http://dailycaller.com/2014/05/05/podesta-congress-cant-stop-obama-on-global-warming/.

7. "all I would say": Darren Goode, "John Podesta: Congress Won't Stop EPA's Climate Rules," *Politico,* May 5, 2014, http://www.politico.com/story/2014/05/john-podesta-epa-congress-106351.html#ixzz31AOSzzjQ.

8. Podesta has been a strong: John Podesta and Sarah Rosen Wartell, "The Power of the President," November 2010, http://www.americanprogress.org/issues/2010/11/pdf/executive_orders.pdf.

9. In the final months: Mike Dorning, "Podesta's Push for Executive Power Raises Stakes on Obama Agenda," Bloomberg.com, December 19, 2013, http://www.bloomberg.com/news/2013-12-20/podesta-s-push-for-executive-power-raises-stakes-on-obama-agenda.html.

10. "The accumulation of all powers": "The Federalist Papers : No. 47," Avalon.Law.Yale.edu, February 1, 1788, http://avalon.law.yale.edu/18th_century/fed47.asp.

11. "When Congress isn't": "Obama: 2014 'Can be a Breakthrough Year' for Economy," UPI.com, January 18, 2014, http://www.upi.com/Top_News/US/2014/01/18/Obama-2014-can-be-a-breakthrough-year-for-economy/UPI-27441390042800/.

12. "We're not just going": Associated Press, "Obama on Executive Actions: 'I've Got a Pen and I've Got a Phone,'" Washington.CBSLocal.com, January 14, 2014, http://washington.cbslocal.com/2014/01/14/obama-on-executive-actions-ive-got-a-pen-and-ive-got-a-phone/.

13. "I taught constitutional": "Obama 2008: 'I Intend to Reverse' Bush Bringing 'More and More Power into the Executive," RealClearPolitics.com, February 13, 2014, http://www.realclearpolitics.com/video/2014/02/13/obama_2008_i_intend_to_reverse_bush_bringing_more_and_more_power_into_the_executive.html.

14. "Before everybody starts:" David Remnick, "Going the Distance," *The New Yorker*, January 24, 2014, http://www.newyorker.com/reporting/2014/01/27/140127fa_fact_remnick?currentPage=all.

15. "I need your help": Elise Foley, "Obama Confronts Hecklers at Immigration Speech," HuffingtonPost.com, November 25, 2013, http://www.huffingtonpost.com/2013/11/25/barack-obama-hecklers-immigration_n_4338945.html.

16. "... if I could solve": Ibid.

17. "to establish a uniform": US Constitution, Article I, Section 8.

18. 43% decrease in: Julia Preston, "Court Deportations Drop 43 Percent in Past Five Years," *The New York Times*, April 16, 2014, http://www. nytimes.com/2014/04/17/us/us-deportations-drop-43-percent-in-last -five-years.html?hpw&rref=us.

19. 1.4 million people: John H. Cushman and Julia Preston, "Obama to Permit Young Migrants to Remain in US," *The New York Times*, June 15, 2012, http://www.nytimes.com/2012/06/16/us/us-to-stop-deporting -some-illegal-immigrants.html?pagewanted=all.

20. "That's the good thing": Daniel Harper, "Obama: I can Do Whatever I Want," *The Weekly Standard*, February 10, 2014, http://www. weeklystandard.com/blogs/obama-thats-good-thing-president-i-can -do-whatever-i-want_778944.html.

21. And while the First: Elizabeth Bumiller, "Inside the Presidency," *National Geographic*, January 2009, http://ngm.nationalgeographic.com/ print/2009/01/president/bumiller-text.

22. "James Madison fashioned": Jonathan Turley, "The President's Power Grab," *Journal Sentinel*, March 15, 2014, http://www.jsonline.com/news/ opinion/the-presidents-power-grab-b99223405z1-250402071.html.

23. "The Framers intended": Andrew P. Naolitano, "Executive Order Tyranny — Obama Plans to Rule America with Pen, Phone," FoxNews. com, February 6, 2014, http://www.foxnews.com/archive/andrew -napolitano/index.html.

24. "unprecedented instruction": Mark Tapscott, "Eric Holder in Hot Water with Federal Judge Over Drug Sentencing Guidelines," WashingtonExaminer.com, April 11, 2014, http://washingtonexaminer .com/eric-holder-in-hot-water-with-federal-judge-over-drug-sentencing -guidelines/article/2547091.

25. "Over the last year": Kelly Riddell, "Holder Bypasses US Sentencing Commission in Mandatory Minimums, Angers US Attorneys," WashingtonExaminer.com, April 10, 2014, http://www.washingtontimes.com/news/2014/apr/10/ holder-bypasses-us-sentencing-commission-mandatory/.

26. "I generally agree": Dan Merica and Evan Perez, "Eric Holder Seeks to Cut Mandatory Minimum Drug Sentences," CNN.com, August 12, 2014, http://www.cnn.com/2013/08/12/politics/holder-mandatory-minimums/.

27. In an astonishing: Ibid.

28. In a February 23: Ibid.

29. "The letter instead": United States v. Windsor, 570 US 12 at 4, 2013.

30. "It is a transparent": Charlie Savage and Cheryl Gay Stolberg, "In Shift, US Says Marriage Act Blocks Gay Rights," New York Times, February 23, 2011, http://www.nytimes.com/2011/02/24/us/24marriage .html?pagewanted=all.

31. A series of frantic: Edward-Isaac Dovere, "Book: How Barack Obama, Eric Holder Agreed on DOMA Plan," Politco.com, April 18, 2014, http://www.politico.com/story/2014/04/barack-obama-eric-holder -defense-of-marriage-act-gay-rights-105794.html.

32. The Justice Department: Sharon Churcher, "Book: Obama Told Advisers to Find 'Way Out' of De-fending DOMA," NewsMax.com, April 18, 2014, http://www.newsmax.com/US/ Obama-Eric-Holder-DOMA-Forcing-the-Spring/2014/04/18/ id/566367#ixzz2zSYY2e2b.

33. "The President expressed": Charlie Savage, "Shift on Executive Power Lets Obama Bypass Congress," *The New York Times*, April 23, 2012, http://www.nytimes.com/2012/04/23/us/politics/shift-on-executive -powers-let-obama-bypass-congress.html?pagewanted=all.

34. "is trying to put": Kelley Riddell, "'High Risk' Label from Feds Puts Gun Sellers in Banks' Crosshairs, Hurts Business," *The Washington Times*, May 18, 2014, http://www.washingtontimes.com/news/2014/may/18/ targeted-gun-sellers-say-high-risk-label-from -feds/?page=1#ixzz32IPLXIqI.

35. "this is an attempt": Ibid.

36. "suggested that it is the": Ibid.

37. According to the Heritage: James L. Gattuso and Diane Katz, "Red Tape Rising: Five Years of Regulatory Expansion," Heritage.org, March 26, 2014, http://www.heritage.org/research/reports/2014/03/ red-tape-rising-five-years-of-regulatory-expansion.

38. Heritage says this: Ibid.

Part I

1. "take care that the": "Take Care Clause," Heritage.org, http://www. heritage.org/constitution/#!/articles/2/essays/98/take-care-clause.

2. "decade-old program": Motoko Rich, "'No Child' Law Whittled Down by White House," *The New York Times,* July 6, 2012, http://www.nytimes. com/2012/07/06/ education/no-child-left-behind-whittled-down -under-obama.html?_r=0.

3. "they must also": Ibid.

4. 17% of our economy: "Why US Spends 17% of GDP on Health Care," JohnTorinus,com, http://johntorinus.com/general-blog/health-care-economics/why-u-s-spends-17-of-gdp-on-health-care/.

5. "with or without": President's State of Union Speech, January 28, 2014.

6. 12,000 inmates in federal: Walter Pavlo, "Here's an Idea to Reduce the Deficit — Release Some Federal Inmates," Forbes.com, February 21, 2013, http://www.forbes.com/sites/walterpavlo/2013/02/21/heres-an-idea-to-reduce-the-deficit-release-some-federal-inmates/.

7. "There are more low-level": Associated Press, "Justice Department Dramatically Expanding Clemency Use," FoxNews.com, January 30, 2014, http://www.foxnews.com/politics/2014/01/30/justice-department-dramatically-expanding-clemency-use/.

8. According to the Bureau: "Recent Trends in the US," BJS.gov, April 2014, http://www.bjs.gov/content/reentry/recidivism.cfm.

9. "the Justice Department": Mike Lillis and Megan R. Wilson, "New Rights for Same-Sex Couples," TheHill.com, February 8, 2014, http://thehill.com/blogs/blog-briefing-room/news/197873-holder-to-extend-same-sex-rights.

10. "the President's authority": Joel Gehrke, "Attorney General Eric Holder Can't Explain Constitutional Basis for Obama's Executive Orders," WashingtonExaminer.com, January 29, 2014, http://washingtonexaminer.com/attorney-general-eric-holder-cant-explain-constitutional-basis-for-obamas-executive-orders/article/2543100.

11. Even in the short: Bryan Llenas, "'Record' Hispanic Voter Turnout in 2012 A Misnomer, Census Numbers Show," FoxNews.com, May 9, 2013, http://latino.foxnews.com/latino/politics/2013/05/09/record-hispanic-voter-turnout-in-2012-myth-census-numbers-show/.

12. While Hispanics are: "Hispanics as a Political Force," Boundless.com, https://www.boundless.com/sociology/understanding-government/the-u-s-political-system/hispanics-as-a-political-force/.

13. In 2012, 66.2%: Sarah Wheaton, "For the First Time on Record, Black Voting Rate Outpaced Rate for Whites in 2012," *The New York Times*, May 8, 2013, http://www.nytimes.com/2013/05/09/us/politics/rate-of-black-voters-surpassed-that-for-whites-in-2012.html.

14. The Census Bureau: "Table 4. Projections of the Population by Sex, Race, and Hispanic Origin for the United States: 2010 to 2050," US Census Bureau. October 24, 2010.

15. Hispanic Vote In Presidential Elections 1980-2012: "Latino Voters in the 2012 Election," PewHispanic.org, November 7, 2012, http://www.

pewhispanic.org/files/2012/11/2012_Latino_vote_exit
_poll_analysis_final_11-07-12.pdf.

16. With about 13%: Associated Press, "Voter Analysis Shows Obama
Would have Lost in 2012 if Black Turnout had Mirrored 2008,"
FoxNews.com, April 28, 2013, http://www.foxnews.com/
politics/2013/04/28/in-first-black-voter-turnout-rate-passes-whites/.

17. To be eligible . . . these requirements: "5 Reasons to Support the Dream
Act," AmericasVoice.org, September 15, 2010, http://americasvoice.org/
research/reasons_to_support_the_dream_act/.

18. In 2012, the United States: "Number of US Deportations,"
StatisticBrain.com, http://www.statisticbrain.com/number-of-u-s-
deportations/.

19. "authorities deported fewer illegal": Stephen Dinan, "Report,
Deportations Plummet in 2013, Lowest Since 2007," *The Washington
Times*, October 30, 2013, http://www.washingtontimes.com/news/2013/
oct/30/deportations-plummet-2013-lowest-2007/?page=all.

20. Only 364,000 were: Ibid.

21. Indeed, Alabama Republican: Matthew Boyle, "Sessions Report
Demolishes Obama 'Deporter in Chief' Myth," Bretibart.com, March
25, 2014, http://www.breitbart.com/Big-Government/2014/03/25/
Sessions-Report-Demolishes-Obama-Deporter-In-Chief-Myth.

22. "more humanely within": Laura Meckler, "Obama Orders
Review of Deportation Practices," *The Wall Street Journal*,
March 13, 2014, http://online.wsj.com/news/articles/
SB10001424052702303546204579438003657934042?mg=reno64- wsj.

23. "emphasized his deep": Kathleen Hennessey and Christi
Parsons, "Obama Orders Deportation Review, Seeks
More Humane Enforcement," *Los Angeles Times*, March
13, 2014, http://articles.latimes.com/2014/mar/13/news/
la-pn-obama-orders-deportation-review-20140313.

24. "a break for businesses": Stephen Dinan, "Obama Eases Penalties
for Businesses Hiring Illegal Immigrants," *The Washington Times*,
February 25, 2014, http://www.washingtontimes.com/news/2014/
feb/25/obama- eases-penalties-for-businesses-hiring- illegal/?
utm_source=RSS_Feed&utm_medium=RSS.

25. "the knowledge that fines": Ibid.

26. Of the 5.8 million: Matt Apuzzo, "Holder Urges States to Lift Bans on
Felons' Voting," *The New York Times*, February 11, 2014,
http://www.nytimes.com/2014/02/12/us/politics/holder
-urges-states-to-repeal-bans-on-voting-byfelons.html.

27. "those swept up": Ibid.

28. no distinction based on race: Hunter v. Underwood, 471 US 222, 232, 1985.

29. Now, Holder is saying: Apuzzo, "Holder Urges States to Lift Bans on Felons' Voting."

30. "at least 341": Ed Barnes, "Felons Voting Illegally May Have Put Franken Over the Top in Minnesota, Study Finds," FoxNews. com, July 12, 2010, http://www.foxnews.com/politics/2010/07/12/felons-voting-illegally-franken-minnesota-study-finds/.

31. "a disparate impact": "Consideration of Arrest and Conviction Records in Employment Decisions Under Title VII of the Civil Right Act of 1964," EEOC.gov, April 25, 2012, http://www.eeoc.gov/laws/guidance/arrest_conviction.cfm.

32. "effectively link specific": Ibid.

33. Indeed, 97% of state: "A System of Plea Bargains," *Los Angeles Times*, March 24, 2012, http://articles.latimes.com/2012/mar/24/opinion/la-ed-plea-bargain-counsel-20120324.

34. Employers who cannot: Byron York, "Should Government Force Businesses to Hire Felons? Obama Nominee Debo Adegbile Says Yes," WashingtonExaminer.com, March 3, 2014, http://washingtonexaminer.com/should-government-force-businesses-to-hire-felons-obama-nominee-debo-adegbile-says-yes/article/2545006.

35. "bright-line policy": "How Widespread is Voter Fraud? | 2012 Facts & Figures," Truethe-Vote.com, http://www.truethevote.org/news/how-widespread-is-voter-fraud-2012-facts-figures.

36. "It's not the people": David Emery, "Stalin: 'It Isn't the People Who Vote that Count,'" UrbanLegends.com, http://urbanlegends.about.com/od/dubiousquotes/a/stalin_quote.htm.

37. Approximately 24 . . . one state: "Inaccurate, Costly, and Inefficient: Evidence that America's Voter Registration System Needs an Upgrade," PewTrusts.org, February 14, 2012, http://www.pewtrusts.org/en/research-and-analysis/reports/2012/02/14/inaccurate-costly-and-inefficient-evidence-that-americas-voter-registration-system-needs-an-upgrade

38. 348,000 deceased individuals: "How Widespread is Voter Fraud? | 2012 Facts & Figures."

39. California: 49,000 . . . Illinois: 24,000: Ibid.

40. "As a result": "Secretary of State Husted to Attorney General Holder: Inconsistent Federal Law Opens Door to Potential Voter Fraud,"

February 10, 2012, http://www.sos.state.oh.us/mediaCenter/
2012/2012-02-10.aspx.

41. By the 2012 . . . numbers too: Zachary Roth, "Voter Fraud in North
     Carolina? Not so Fast," MSNBC.com, April 8, 2014, http://www.msnbc.
     com/msnbc/voter-fraud-north-carolina-not-so-fast-0.

42. The Richardson . . . as well: John Fund, "The Voter Fraud That
     'Never Happens' Keeps Coming Back," NationalReview.com,
     February 8, 2013, http://www.nationalreview.com/corner/340174/
     voter-fraud-never-happens-keeps-coming-back-john-fund.

43. Thirty-two million votes: "2012 Early Voting Statistics," November 6,
     2012, http://elections.gmu.edu/early_vote_2012.html.

44. In the state's: Ray C. Bliss, "A Study of Early Voting in Ohio Elections,"
     University of Akron, UAkron.edu, https://www.uakron.edu/bliss/
     research/archives/2010/EarlyVotingReport.pdf.

45. 43% of early voters: Ibid.

46. "white devil . . . cracker": John Fund, "Holder's Black Panther
     Stonewall," *The Wall Street Journal,* August 20, 2009, http://
     online.wsj.com/news/articles/SB10001424052970203550
     604574361071968458430.

47. In April, 2009: Ibid.

48. "though it had basically": "Editorial: Return of the Black Panther,"
     The Washington Times, July 7, 2009, http://www.washingtontimes.com/
     news/2009/jul/07/return-of-the-black-panther/.

49. reverse the *Citizens United* decision: Gabriel Debenetti, "US Senate
     to Vote this Year on Campaign Finance Amendment: Schumer,"
     Reuters, April 14, 2014, http://www.reuters.com/article/2014/04/30/
     us-usa-campaign-finance-idUSBREA3T0N620140430.

50. "the worst decision": Dave Levinthal and Anna Palmer, "Schumer,
     Dems Vilify Citizens United Decision," *Politico,* April 18, 2012, http://
     www.politico.com/politicoinfluence/0412/politicoinfluence243.html.

51. Schumer, along with: Becket Adams, "Chuck Schumer Call on IRS
     to Crack Down on Tea Party Funding: 'Redouble those Efforts
     Immediately,'" TheBlaze.com, January 14, 2014, http://
     www.theblaze.com/stories/2014/01/24/chuck-schumer-calls-for
     -irs-to-crack-down-on-tea-party-funding/.

52. Schumer urged the Obama: Ibid.

53. "but there are": Ibid.

54. "there continues to be": Associated Press, "IRS Moves to Limit
     Tax-Exempt Groups After Targeting Scandal," FoxNews.com,

November 27, 2013, http://www.foxnews.com/politics/2013/11/27/irs-pushes-to-rein-in-tax-exempt-political-groups.

55. "As a 501(c)(4)": E-mail from Jenny Beth Martin to Dick Morris, February 2, 2014.

56. What are your . . . Explain: Dick Morris, "The IRS Audit from Hell," http://www.realclearpolitics.com/articles/2013/05/22/the_irs_audit_from_hell__118502.html.

57. 10% of the: Stephen Dinan, "House Republicans Find 10% of Tea Party Donors Audited by IRS," *The Washington Times*, May 7, 2014, http://www.washingtontimes.com/news/2014/may/7/house-republicans-find-10-of-tea-party-donors- audi/?page=all.

58. "will stifle political": E-mail from Rob Boysen to Dick Morris, January 30, 2014.

59. "a blatant attempt": Ibid.

60. "voter registration activities": Maria Barron, "Letters: IRS Stifling Free Speech," HillCountryNews.com, February 19, 2014, http://www.hillcountrynews.com/opinion/letters_to_editor/article_8b7903bc-998a-11e3-8db8-001a4bcf887a.html?mode=print.

61. "curtail activities such": Associated Press, "IRS Moves to Limit Tax-Exempt Groups After Targeting Scandal."

62. "the ruling of the": Associated Press, "IRS Moves to Limit Tax-Exempt Groups After Targeting Scandal."

63. "to hold those . . . decades old": Associated Press, "IRS Moves to Limit Tax-Exempt Groups After Targeting Scandal."

64. "If treasury and the IRS": Patrick Howley, "Email: IRS's Lerner, Treasury Department Secretly Drafted New Rules to Restrict Nonprofits," DialyCaller.com, February 5, 2014, http://dailycaller.com/2014/02/05/email-irss-lerner-treasury-department-secretly-drafted-new-rules-to-re-strict-nonprofits/#ixzz2sY4lFhzl.

65. "has absolutely no": Michael Cieply and Nicholas Confessore, "Leaning Right in Hollywood, Under a Lens," *The New York Times*, January 22, 2014, http://www.nytimes.com/2014/01/23/us/politics/leaning-right-in-hollywood-under-a-lens.html.

66. The IRS eventually: "No Shield from Scrutiny for the IRS in O'Donnell Case," *The Washington Times*, January 28, 2014, http://www.washingtontimes.com/news/2014/jan/28/editorial-no-shield-for-the-irs/?utm_source=RSS_Feed&utm_medium=RSS.

67. Mrs. O'Donnell, this is: Dave Boyer and Ben Wolfgang, "Former GOP Senate Candidate Chris-tine O'Donnell Told Her Tax Records Were Breached," *The Washington Times*, July 17, 2013, http://www.washingtontimes.com/news/2013/jul/17/former-gop-senate-candidate-christine-odonnell-tol/?page=all.

68. Because the access: Dave Boyer, "Delaware Officials Admit Tax Snooping; Won't Identify Christine O'Donnell as Target," *The Washington Times*, July 19, 2013, http://www.washingtontimes.com/news/2013/jul/19/delware-officials- admit-snooping-gop-candidate-chr/?page=all.

69. "about state investigator": Ibid.

70. "routinely compares states": Ibid.

71. "The state [of Delaware]": Ibid.

72. "House Oversight Committee": Seth McLaughlin, "Records of Christine O'Donnell Tax Snoop-ing Disappear," *The Washington Times*, July 23, 2013, http://www.washingtontimes.com/news/2013/jul/23/records-of-christine-odonnell-tax-snooping-disappe/?page=all.

73. "even Ms. O'Donnell": Ibid.

74. the only two people: Ibid.

75. "unauthorized access or": Dave Boyer and Ben Wolfgang, "Exclusive: Feds Admit Improper Scrutiny of Candidate, Donor Tax Records," *The Washington Times*, July 15, 2013, http://www.washingtontimes.com/news/2013/jul/15/feds-admit-improper-scrutiny-candidate-donor-tax-r/.

76. "somebody did this": Stephen Dinan, "Marriage Group to Sue IRS Over Donor Leak, Says List Went to Political Enemies," *The Washington Times*, October 3, 2013, http://www.washingtontimes.com/ news/2013/oct/3/marriage-group-to-sue-irs-over-donor-leak/?page=all.

77. "suggests to me": Ibid.

78. "had their tax": E-mail from source to Dick Morris, February 1, 2014.

79. Adelson, reputed to . . . against him: Luisa Kroll, "Billionaire Sheldon Adelson was Year's Biggest Winner, with Fortune Jumping $15 Billion," *Forbes*, December 23, 2013, http://www.forbes.com/sites/luisakroll/2013/12/23/billionaire-sheldon-adelson-was-years-biggest-winner-with-fortune-jumping-15-billion/.

80. An IRS audit . . . its payroll: Bill Allison, "Gingrich Super PAC Super Donor Sheldon Adelson has Businesses Under Scrutiny by IRS, Justice," SunlightFoundation.com, January 26, 2012, http://sunlightfoundation.com/blog/2012/01/26/adelson-sands/.

81. "I have heard": Mackenzie Weinger, "Ted Cruz Spars with Eric Holder at IRS Targeting Hearing," FoxNews.com, January 1, 2014, http://nation.foxnews.com/2014/01/29/ ted- cruz-spars-eric- holder-irs-targeting-hearing.

82. "a bitter foe": Becket Adams, "Romney Donor Finds Out What it Means to Be on President Obama's 'Enemies List,'" TheBlaze.com, May 11, 2012, http://www.theblaze.com/stories/2012/05/11/romney-donor -finds-out-what-it-means-to-be-on-president-obamas-enemies-list/.

83. The Wall Street: "Strassel: Trolling for Dirt on the President's List," *The Wall Street Journal*, May 10, 2012, http://online.wsj.com/news/articles/ SB10001424052702304070304577396412560038208.

84. "We literally do have": "The Obama Regime DOJ's Harassment of Fox News Ties into the IRS Attack on Republican Donors," RushLimbaugh. com, May 20, 2013, http://www.rushlimbaugh.com/daily/2013/05/20/ the_obama_regime_doj_s_harassment_of_fox_news_ties_into_the_irs _attack_on_republican_donors.

85. "The word's out": Alex Pappas, "Did the IRS Give Mitt Romney's Tax Returns to Harry Reid?" DailyCaller.com, May 16, 2013, http://dailycaller.com/2013/05/16/did-the-irs-give-romneys-tax -returns-to-harry-reid/.

86. rose by 41%: "America's Entitlement Budget Disaster," USAGovPolicy.com, October 14, 2013, http://www.usagovpolicy.com/ nyanalysis/americas-entitlement-budget-disaster/.

87. Today the 83 . . . per year: "CRS Report: Welfare Spending the Largest Item in the Federal Budget," Budget.Senate.gov, October 18, 2012, http://www.budget.senate.gov/republican/public/index.cfm/ budget-background?ID=3c687e99-a5c5-46f2-9f9d-0ea5a62c3183.

88. "There are 47 percent": Josh Voorhees, "Mitt Romney is Still Trying, Failing, to Explain Away his "47 Percent" Remarks,"Slate.com, July 29, 2013, http://www.slate.com/blogs/the_slatest/2013/07/29/ mitt_romney_on_mojo_s_47_percent_tape_actually_i_didn_t_say_that_ about_personal.html.

89. According to the Census: Terence P. Jeffrey, "Census Bureau: Means-Tested Gov't Benefit Recipients Outnumber Full-Time Year-Round Workers," CNSNews.com, October 24, 2013, http://cnsnews.com/news/ article/terence-p-jeffrey/census-bureau-means-tested-govt-benefit -recipients-outnumber-full.

90. 60% of all Americans: "America's Entitlement Budget Disaster."

91. During Obama's first: "Enrollment in Federal Social Welfare Programs Outpaces Job Growth in Last 4 Years," FoxNews.com, October 10, 2012, http://nation.foxnews.com/social-welfare/2012/10/10/enrollment-federal-social-welfare-programs-outpaces-job-growth-last-4-years.

92. Means Tested Government Programs, 2011: Jeffrey, "Census Bureau: Means-Tested Gov't Benefit Recipients Outnumber Full-Time Year-Round Workers."

93. almost one trillion: Jess Sessions, "CRS Report: Welfare Spending the Largest Item in the Federal Budget," Budget.Senate.gov, http://www.budget.senate.gov/republican/public/index.cfm/files/serve/?File_id=34919307-6286-47ab-b114-2fd5bcedfeb5.

94. The exclusively federal: Ibid.

95. 27 million Americans: Brad Plumer, "Why are 47 Million Americans on Food Stamps? It's the Recession — Mostly." *The Washington Post*, September 23, 2013, http://www.washingtonpost.com/blogs/wonkblog/wp/2013/09/23/why-are-47-million-americans-on-food-stamps-its-the-recession-mostly/.

96. Thirty percent have: "Policy Basics: Introductino to the Supplemental Nutrition Assistance Program (SNAP)," CBPP.org, March 19, 2014, http://www.cbpp.org/cms/index.cfm?fa=view&id=2226.

97. 5.4 million Americans: John Merline, "$5.4 Million Join Disability Rolls Under Obama," Investor's Business Daily, April 20, 2012, http://news.investors.com/business/042012-608418-ssdi-disability-rolls-skyrocket-under-obama.htm?p=full.

98. "relaxation of the medical": Avik Roy, "How Americans Gave the $200 Billion-a-Year 'Disability-Industrial Complex,'" Forbes.com, April 8, 2013, http://www.forbes.com/sites/theapothecary/2013/04/08/how-americans-game-the-200-billion-a-year-disability-industrial-complex/.

99. 50 million enrollees: Eileen Ellis, Dennis Roberts, Laura Snyder and Robin Rudowitz, "Medicaid En-rollment: June 2012 Data Snapshot," KFF.org, August 21, 2013, http://kff.org/medicaid/issue-brief/medicaid-enrollment-june-2012-data-snapshot/.

100. 3 million more: Dan Mangan, "Medicaid Enrollment Jumps by 3 Million Under Obamacare," CNBC.com, April 4, 2014, http://www.cnbc.com/id/101555492.

101. 8 million people: "Appendix B, Updated Estimates of the Insurance Coverage Provisions of the Afford-able Care Act," CBO.gov, http://www.cbo.gov/sites/default/files/cbofiles/attachments/45010-breakout-AppendixB.pdf.

102. With only forty . . . earlier years": James Bovard, "The Food-Stamp Crime Wave," Wall Street Journal, June 23, 2011, http://online.wsj.com/news/articles/SB10001424052702304657804576401412033504294.

103. "The Milwaukee Journal": Ibid.

104. "A Seattle recipients": Ibid.

105. "Thirty percent of the": Ibid.

106. New York City's Human Resources": Ibid.

107. Nine Milwaukee, WI: Ibid.

108. "the Obama administration: Ibid.

109. "After Mr. Fick: Ibid.

110. cost taxpayers $400 million: Damien Paletta and Pervaiz Shallwani, "NYPD Cops, Firefighters Charged with Disability Fraud," Wall Street Journal, January 8, 2014, http://online.wsj.com/news/articles/SB10001424052702303933104579306270271026090.

111. "the plot, allegedly": Ibid.

112. "coached the applicants": Ibid.

113. "It maintains our commitment": Roy, "How Americans Gave the $200 Billion-a-Year 'Disability-Industrial Complex.'"

114. the overall effect was to: Ibid.

115. "replace the majority": Ibid.

116. as much as 20%: Ibid.

117. 46.4% of Americans: Lucy Madison, "Fact-Checking Romney's '47 Percent' Comment," CBSNews.com, September 25, 2012, http://www.cbsnews.com/news/fact-checking-romneys-47-percent-comment/.

118. Half of those . . . no income taxes: Ibid.

119. Only 18%: Ibid.

120. Today 37.2 . . . took office: Tyler Durden, "People Not in Labor Force Soar to Record 91.8 Million; Participation Rate Plunges to 1978 Levels," ZeroHedge.com, January 10, 2014, http://www.zerohedge.com/news/2014-01-10/people-not-labor-force-soar-record-918-million-participation-rate-plunges-1978-level.

121. Senate has refused: "Nominations," senate.gov, http://www.senate.gov/artandhistory/history/common/briefing/Nominations.htm#9.

122. Obama has only . . . of the time: Federal Judicial Nominee Confirmation Percentage, JudicialNomina-tions.org, http://www.judicialnominations.org/wp-content/uploads/2014/01/Federal-Confirmation-Percentage-1.2.2014.jpg.

123. 95 were vacant: "Judicial Vacancies," AmericanBar.com, http://www.americanbar.org/advocacy/governmental_legislative_work/priorities_policy/independence_of_the_judiciary/judicial_vacancies.html.

124. Senate Republican leader: Paul Kane, "Reid, Democrats Trigger 'Nuclear' Option; Eliminate Most Filibusters on Nominees," *The Washington Post*, November 21, 2013, http://www.washingtonpost.com/politics/senate-poised-to-limit-filibusters-in- party-line-vote-that-would-alter-centuries-of-precedent/2013/11/21/d065cfe8-52b6-11e3-9fe0-fd2ca728e67c_story.html.

125. "It's another raw": Ibid.

126. "that if you talk . . . the government": Ravi Somaiya, "Head of the A.O. Criticizes Seizure of Phone Records," *The New York Times*, May 19, 2013, http://www.nytimes.com/2013/05/20/business/media/head-of-the-ap- criticizes-seizure-of-phone-records.html.

127. "limited and biased": Ibid.

128. "There can be no": Sari Horwitz, "Under Sweeping Subpoenas, Justice Department Obtained AP Phone Records in Leak Investigation," *The Washington Post*, May 13, 2013, http://www.washingtonpost.com/world/national-security/under-sweeping- subpoenas-justice-department-obtained-ap-phone-records-in-leak-investigation/2013/05/13/11d1bb82- bc11-11e2-89c9-3be8095fe767_story.html.

129. "intelligence services detected." Ibid.

130. "said that it had": Ibid.

131. "I am convinced": HuffingtonPost.com, October 15, 2008, http://www.huffingtonpost.com/2008/10/15/obama-if-i-were- watching_n_135033.html.

132. "ultimately destructive for": Brian Stelter, "Obama Says Fox News Promotes 'Destructive' Viewpoint," MediaDecoder.com, September 28, 2010, http://mediadecoder.blogs.nytimes.com/2010/09/28/obama-says-fox-news-promotes-destructive-viewpoint/.

133. "If you talk to": Andrew Johnson, "Obama Targets Fow News, GOC for Obamacare Glitches," NationalReview.com, September 26, 2013, http://www.nationalreview.com/corner/359591/obama-targets-fox-news-gop-obamacare-glitches-andrew-johnson.

134. "if a Republican member": Franklin Foer and Chris Hughes, "Barack Obama is Not Pleased," NewRepublic.com, http://www.newrepublic.com/article/112190/obama-interview-2013-sit-down-president#.

135. On October 23: Josh Feldman, "Fox's Beckel Reveals White House 'Bludgeoned' Him for Speaking Out on Delaying Obamacare,"

Mediaite.com, October 23, 2013, http://www.mediaite.com/tv/
foxs-beckel-reveals-white-house-bludgeoned-him-for-speaking-out
-on-delaying-obamacare/.

136. "I'm not the caricature": Franklin Foer and Chris Hughes, "Barack
Obama is Not Pleased," NewRepublic.com, January 27, 2013, http://
www.newrepublic.com/article/112190/obama-interview-2013-sit
-down-president#.Deco MediaDecocoak Investigation,tigation
„igation„„rew-johnson..ediaite.com/online/obama-im-not-the
-caricature-that-you-see-on-fox-news-or-rush-limbaugh/.

137. "these kinds of things . . . ": Dominic Patten, "UPDATE: Obama Slams
'Successful' Fox News Again in Taped
O'Reilly Interview," Deadline.com, February 3, 2014, http://
www.deadline.com/2014/02/super-bowl-obama-oreilly-interview/.

138. While 75% of: Survey by National Center for Survey Research,
November 29, 2010.

139. The Nielsen ratings: Nielsen ratings for January, 2014.

140. A survey . . . television network: Mark Guarino, "Flash! Fox News is the
Most Trusted Net-work . . . and the Least Trusted," CSMonitor.com,
January 31, 2014, http://www.csmonitor.com/USA/Society/2014/0131/
Flash!- Fox-News-is-the-most-trusted-network-and- the-least-trusted.

141. "most transparent administration": Jonathan Easley, "Obama Says His
is 'Most Transparent Administration' Ever," TheHill.com, February
14, 2013, http://thehill.com/blogs/blog-briefing-room/news/283335-
obama-this-is-the-most-transparent-administration-in-history.

142. "Unlike media photographers": Ron Fournier, "Obama's Image
Machine: Monopolistic Propaganda Funded by You," NationalJournal
.com, November 21, 2013, http://www.nationaljournal.com/pictures
-video/obama-s-image- machine-monopolistic-propaganda- funded-by
-you-20131121.

143. "you guys are just like": Ibid.

144. "Obama's image-makers": Ibid.

145. "As surely as . . . newsgathering activities": Ibid.

146. "FCC [has] proposed": Ajit Pai, "The FCC Wades Into the Newsroom,"
The Wall Street Journal, February 10, 2014, http://online.wsj.com/news/
articles/SB10001424052702304680904579366903828260732.

147. The purpose of CIN: Ibid.

148. The FCC planned: Chris Whittington, "Obama, FCC to Openly Monitor
News Outlets," VicksburgDailyNews.com, February 20, 2014, http://
www.fcc.gov/document/ocbo-announces-release-critical-information
-needs-research-design.

149. "they would be out": Pai, "The FCC Wades Into the Newsroom."

150. dropped from 35%: "Union Members — 2013," BLS.gov, January 24, 2013, http://www.bls.gov/news.release/pdf/union2.pdf.

151. unions won 64%: Michael Paarlberg, "The NLRB's Bid to Remain Relevant," *The Guardian*, July 1, 2011, http://www.theguardian.com/commentisfree/cifamerica/2011/jul/01/nlrb-boeing-unions.

152. 626 voting yes: Steven Greenhouse, "U.A.W. Asks Labor Board to Examine Vote at Tennessee Plant," *The New York Times*, February 21, 2014, http://www.nytimes.com/2014/02/22/business/uaw-asks-labor -board-to-examine-vote-at-tennessee-plant.html.

153. "overstepped his bounds": Associated Press, "Supreme Court Justices Call into Question Obama's Recess Appointment Power," FoxNews. com, January 20, 2014, http://www.foxnews.com/politics/2014/01/13/ supreme-court-justices-call-into-question-obama-recess-appointment -power/.

154. "suggested that it is the": Ibid.

155. "this ambush election . . . Big Labor": John Kline, "Kline, Roe Respond to NLRB's Ambush Election Rule," EdWorkforce.house.gov, February 5, 2014, http://edworkforce.house.gov/news/documentsingle.aspx ?DocumentID=368959.

156. saved $2 billion: Steven Greenhouse, "Wisconsin's Legacy for Unions," *The New York Times*, February 22,2014, http://www.nytimes.com/2014/ 02/23/business/wisconsins-legacy-for-unions.html.

157. Of the 400 unions: Ibid.

158. drop from 1,000 to: Ibid.

159. "It just spread": Lydia Depillis, "Auto Union Loses Historic Election at Volkswagen Plant in Tennessee," *The Washington Post,* February 14, 2014, http://www.washingtonpost.com/blogs/wonkblog/wp/2014/02/14/ united-auto-workers-lose-historic-election-at-chattanooga -volkswagen-plant/.

160. "employees right to": Shiloh D. Theberge, Fisher & Phillips, "Employers be Aware: National Labor Relations Board Turns Focus to Nonunionized Workplaces," BandgoDailyNews.com, February 14, 2014, http://bangordailynews.com/2014/02/14/business/employers -be-aware-national-labor-relations-board-turns-focus-to -nonunionized-workplaces/.

161. "Confidentiality policies . . . appropriate conduct": Ibid.

162. "President Obama has given": Jeffrey T. Kuhner, "KEHNER: Obama's Power Grab," *The Washington Times*, March 22, 2012, http://www. washingtontimes.com/news/2012/mar/22/obamas-power-grab/.

163. "stunning in its audacity": Ibid.

164. "federal government has the": Ibid.

165. "the United States": Ibid.

166. The Secretary of . . . of energy: Jim Garrison, "Martial Law by Executive Order," HuffingtonPost.com, March 21, 2012, http://www.huffingtonpost.com/jim-garrison/martial-law-under-another_b_1370819.html.

167. "a fairly standard": "'The Real Obama": Absolute Power," FoxNews.com, March 20, 2013, http://nation.foxnews.com/sean-hannity/2012/03/20/real-obama-absolute-power.

Part II

1. $3 trillion in taxes: Richard Rubin, "Wealthiest Pay Higher Taxes with Scant US Economic Harm," Bloomberg.com, April 11, 2014, http://www.bloomberg.com/news/2014-04-11/wealthiest-pay-higher-taxes-with-scant-u-s-economic-harm.html.

2. cost another $1.9 trillion: "Regulator Without Peer," *The Wall Street Journal*, April 16, 2014, http://online.wsj.com/news/articles/SB10001424052702304311204579505953682216682.

Chapter 1

1. "For 46 hours": Carrie Budoff Brown, "Lawmakers Challenged To Read Health Care Bill Before Voting," Politico.com, June 30, 2009, http://www.politico.com/news/stories/0609/24348_Page2.html.

2. more than 17%: Robert Reiss, "Visionary Healthcare Leader Series, Interview #2 Dr. Raymond J. Baxter from Kaiser Permanente," Forbes.com, March 18, 2014, http://www.forbes.com/sites/robertreiss/2014/03/18/visionary-healthcare-leader-series-interview-2-dr-raymond-j-baxter-from-kaiser-permanente/.

3. "But we have to": Jonathan Capehart, "Pelosi Defends Her Infamous Health Care Remark," *The Washington Post*, June 20, 2012, http://www.washingtonpost.com/blogs/post-partisan/post/pelosi-defends-her-infamous-health-care-remark/2012/06/20/gJQAqch6qV_blog.html.

4. David Gregory . . . get it done: "David Gregory Asks Pelosi About 'Pass the Bill so You Can Find Out What's in it' Policy," RealClearPolitics.com, http://www.realclearpolitics.com/video/2013/11/17/david_gregory_asks_pelosi_about_pass_the_bill_so_you_can_find_out_whats_in_it_comment.html.

5.   961 pages — 397 words: Susan Jones, "Sebelius on Obamacare
     Regulations: 'I Don't Know How Many Pages,'" CNSNews.com,
     December 12, 2013, http://cnsnews.com/news/article/susan-jones/
     sebelius-obamacare-regulations-i-dont-know-how-many-pages.

6.   10,535 pages, or about: Ibid.

7.   By the end of 2013: Glenn Kessler, "How Many Pages of Regulations
     for 'Obamacare'?", WashingtonPost.com, May 15, 2013, http://www.
     washingtonpost.com/blogs/fact-checker/post/how-many-pages-of
     -regulations-for-obamacare/2013/05/14/61eec914-bcf9-11e2-9b09
     -1638acc3942e_blog.html.

8.   "a third of all of the:" Melissa Clyne, "White House Failed
     to Review Many Obamacare Regulations," NewsMax.com,
     December 6, 2013, http://www.newsmax.com/Newsfront/
     obamacare-mistakes-regulations-review/2013/12/06/id/540366.

9.   democratic senators . . .Whitehouse (D-RI): Byron York, "27
     Democratic Senators Who Promised You Could Keep Your Health
     Coverage," WashingtonExaminer.com, November 15, 2013, http://
     washingtonexaminer.com/27-democratic-senators-who-promised
     -you-could-keep-your-health-coverage/article/2539245.

10. "If you don't have health": Barack Obama, "Why We Need Health Care
     Reform," *The New York Times*, August 15, 2009, http://
     www.nytimes.com/2009/08/16/opinion/16obama.html.

11. "lie of the year": Angie Drobnic Holan, "Lied of the Year: 'If You Like
     Your Health Care Plan, You Can Keep it'," PolitiFact.com, December 12,
     2013, http://www.politifact.com/truth-o-meter/article/2013/dec/12/
     lie-year-if-you-like-your-health-care-plan-keep-it/.

12. "employers or issuers": D'Angelo Gore, "Fact Check: If You Like
     Your Health Plan, You Can Keep it," USAToday.com, November 11,
     2013, http://www.usatoday.com/story/news/politics/2013/11/11/
     fact-check-keeping-your-health-plan/3500187/.

13. "However, if health plans": Ibid.

14. "Bottom line is that": Ibid.

15. 4.8 million Americans: Avik Roy, "The Obamacare Exchange
     Scorecard: Around 100,000 Enrollees and Five Million Cancellations,"
     Forbes.com, November 12, 2013, http://www.forbes.com/sites/
     theapothecary/2013/11/12/the-obamacare-exchange-scorecard
     -around-100000-enrollees-and-five-million-cancellations/.

16. "I am sorry . . . for this": Ashley Killough, "Obama Apologizes
     for Insurance Cancellations Due to Obamacare," CNN.com,
     November 7, 2013, http://www.cnn.com/2013/11/07/politics/
     obama-obamacare-apology/.

17. "was not precise enough": Chris Stirewalt, "It's Not a Broken Promise if You Never Meant to Keep it," FoxNews.com, October 30, 2013, http://www.foxnews.com/politics/2013/10/30/its-not-broken-promise-if-never-meant-to-keep-it/.

18. "because of the normal": Lisa Myers and Hannah Rappleye, "Obama Admin. Knew Millions Could Not Keep their Health Insurance," NBCNews.com, October 28, 2013, http://www.nbcnews.com/news/other/obama-admin-knew-millions-could-not-keep-their-health-insurance-f8C11484394.

19. involving only 5%: Avik Roy, "Obama Officials in 2010: 93 Million Americans Will be Unable to Keep Their Health Plans Under Obamacare," Forbes.com, October 12, 2013, http://www.forbes.com/sites/theapothecary/2013/10/31/obama-officials-in-2010-93-million-americans-will-be-unable-to-keep-their-health-plans-under-obamacare/.

20. "The Department's mid-range": Ibid.

21. The CNN poll: Daniel Doherty, "CNN Poll: Obama's Honesty and Trustworthiness Numbers Take a Huge Hit," Townhall.com, November 25, 2013, http://townhall.com/tipsheet/danieldoherty/2013/11/25/poll-obamas-honesty-and-trustworthiness-numbers-upside-down-n1752799.

22. "What we said was": "Obama: 'What we Said was You Can Keep it if it Hasn't Changed Since the Law Passed,'" FoxNews.com, http://nation.foxnews.com/2013/11/05/obama-what-we-said-was-you-can-keep-it-if-it-hasnt-changed-law-passed.

23. "four Pinocchios for": Ron Fournier, "Lying About Lies: Why Credibility Matters to Obama," NationalJournal.com, November 5, 2013, http://www.nationaljournal.com/white-house/lying-about-lies-why-credibility-matters-to-obama-20131105.

24. "orchestrated deceit": Ibid.

25. On November 14, 2013: Liz Goodwin and Olivier Knox, "Obama Announces 'Keep Your Plan' Obamacare Fix," Yahoo.com, November 14, 2013, http://news.yahoo.com/obama-to-make-obamacare-statement-at-11-35-a-m-145708141.html.

26. So just before . . . age of thirty": Sally Pipes, "The Obamacare Law Devours Itself with Exemptions Amid 5 Million (and Counting) Cancellations," Forbes.com, January 6, 2014, http://www.forbes.com/sites/sallypipes/2014/01/06/the-obamacare-law-devours-itself-with-exemptions-amid-5-million-and-counting-cancellations/.

27. only 2.6 million previously: Avik Roy, "New McKinsey Survey: 74% of Obamacare Sign-Ups Were Previously Insured," Forbes.com, May 10, 2014, http://www.forbes.com/sites/theapothecary/2014/05/10/new-mckinsey-survey-74-of-obamacare-sign-ups-were-previously-insured/.

28. White House claimed that: "White House Report Confirms 8 Million Obamacare Enrollees," US-News.com, May 1, 2014, http://health.usnews.com/health-news/articles/2014/05/01/white-house-report-confirms-8-million-obamacare-enrollees.

29. Only 26% of those: Roy, "New McKinsey Survey: 74% of Obamacare Sign-Ups Were Previously Insured."

30. 5.5% of the 36 million: Mollyann Brodie, Jamie Firth and Liz Hamel, "Kaiser Health Tracking Poll: April 2014," KFF.org, April 29, 2014, http://kff.org/health-reform/poll-finding/kaiser-health-tracking-poll-april-2014/?__hstc=87270983.02eb520ce6251feb703451e1254ab20f.1397855146974.1398789572796.1398795820712.11&__hssc=87270983.2.1398795820712&__hsfp=3266777509.

31. "through an Exchange": Chris Casteel, "Lawsuits By Oklahoma Attorney General Scott Pruitt, Others Challenge Obamacare Subsidies," *The Oklahoman*, December 5, 2013, http://newsok.com/lawsuits-by-oklahoma-attorney-general-scott-pruitt-others-challenge-obamacare-subsidies/article/3911239.

32. thirty-four states opted not: Ibid.

33. "There is evidence": Reuters, "US Judge Rejects Challenge to Obamacare Insurance Subsidies," CNBC.com, January 15, 2014, http://www.cnbc.com/id/101339123.

34. "In Senate Finance": George F. Will, "Obamacare's Four-Work Achilles Heel," *The New York Post*, January 31, 2014, http://nypost.com/2014/01/31/obamacares-four-word-achilles-heel/.

35. Unilateral Changes in Affordable Care Act: Tyler Hartsfield and Grace-Marie Turner, "40 Changes to Obamacare . . . So Far," reprinted by permission of the Galen Institute, Galen.org, April 8, 2014, http://www.galen.org/newsletters/changes-to-obamacare-so-far/.

36. 97 percent of the new jobs: Kevin G. Hall, "Most 2013 Job Growth is in Part-Time Work, Survey Suggests," McClatchyDC.com, August 2, 2013, http://www.mcclatchydc.com/2013/08/02/198432/most-2013-job-growth-is-in-part.html.

37. 963,000 more people: Ibid.

38. "That is a really high": Ibid.

39. "employers are trying": Alex Rogers, "Labor Leader Admits ObamaCare Woes," Time.com, August 29, 2013, http://swampland.time.com/2013/08/29/labor-leader-admits-obamacare-woes/.

40. "continuing failure to faithfully": Tom Tillison, "30 Congressmen Sign Resolution to Sue Obama for 'Failure to Faithfully Execute the Laws,'" bizpacreview.com, December 13, 2013, http://www.bizpacreview .com/2013/12/13/30-congressmen-sign-resolution-to-sue-obama -for-failure-to-faithfully-execute-the-laws-88898.

41. The big problem: Josh Israel, "30 Members of Congress Want the House of Representatives to Sure Obama," ThinkProgress.org, December 17, 2013, http://thinkprogress.org/ justice/2013/12/17/3075371/30-house-republicans-obamacare-suit/.

42. "to pick and choose": Ibid.

43. "take care that the laws": Sai Prakash, "Take Care Clause," Heritage.org, http://www.heritage.org/constitution/#!/articles/ 2/essays/98/take-care-clause.

44. Members of Congress get paid $174,000 per year: Jane C. Timm, "Congressman: We're Underpaid!" MSNBC.com, April 4, 2014, http:// www.msnbc.com/msnbc/congress-underpaid-moran.

45. under 400 percent: Bill Cassidy, "No Congressional Obamacare Exemptions," TheHill.com, September 30, 2013, http://thehill.com/blogs/congress-blog/ healthcare/325201-no-congressional-obamacare-exemptions.

46. "by arranging for members": Ron Johnson, "I'm Suing Over Obamacare Exemptions for Congress," *The Wall Street Journal*, January 6, 2014, http://online.wsj.com/news/articles/SB10001424052702304325004579 296140856419808.

47. "During the drafting": Ibid.

48. "essentially declared the federal": Ibid.

49. "We have to pass": Capehart, "Pelosi Defends Her Infamous Health Care Remark."

Chapter 2

1. For a discussion of Nevada's critics of Common Core see: http://www.lasvegassun.com/news/2014/apr/22/ state-lawmakers-hear-pros-cons-common-core-curricu/.

2. Stanley Kurtz, author of: Stanley Kurtz, "Should the White House Control What Your Kids Learn in School," FoxNews.com, September 7, 2012, http://www.foxnews.com/opinion/2012/09/07/ should-white-house-control-what-your-kids-learn-in-school/.

3. "has grown more": Ibid.

4. "the hard left's": Ibid.

5.   "(1a) a politicized . . . urban schools.": Ibid.

6. $600 billion spent: "Per Student Public Education Spending Decreases in 2011 for First Time in Nearly Four Decades, Census Bureau Reports," Census.gov, May 21, 2013, http://www.census.gov/newsroom/releases/archives/governments/cb13-92.html.

7.   "eliminates local control": Student Public Education Spending Decreaslehind the Curtain of Hidden Language, LanristianPost.com, March 18, 2013, http://www.christianpost.com/news/common-core-cirriculum-a-look-behind-the- curtain-of-hidden-language-92070/.

8.   "by an organization": Ibid.

9.   "driven by policymakers": Ibid.

10.   supporters of Achieve: Our Contributors, Achieve.org, http://www.achieve.org/contributors.

11.   "the standards better": Valerie Strauss, "Chicago Teachers Union Passes Resolution Opposing Common Core," *The Washington Post*, May 9, 2014, http://www.washingtonpost.com/blogs/answer-sheet/wp/2014/05/09/chicago-teachers-union-passes-resolution-opposing-common-core/?wpisrc=nl_headlines.

12.   The Common Core curriculum: Alexander, "Common Core Curriculum: A Look Behind the Curtain of Hidden Language."

13.   In a recent example: "Kid Misses Common Core Math Problems Because he Didn't Use 'Friendly' Numbers," March 25, 2014, http://twitchy.com/2014/03/25/kid-misses-common-core-math-problems-because-he-didnt-use-friendly-numbers-pic/.

14.   James Milgram, Mathematics: Alexander, "Common Core Curriculum: A Look Behind the Curtain of Hidden Language."

15.   "de-emphasizes the study": Ibid.

16.   21st Century competencies": Joy Pullmann, "Joy Pullmann: Data Mining Kids Crosses Line," Orange County Register, August 21, 2013, http://www.ocregister.com/articles/data-499062-schools-information.html.

17. $5 billion for funds: Caitlin Emma, "Time, Not Money, at Issue for Race to Top States," Politico.com, March 19, 2014, http://www.politico.com/story/2014/03/race-to-the-top-reports-education-104808.html.

18.   "No one debated": Allie Bidwell, "The Politics of Common Core," USNews.com, March 6, 2014, http://www.usnews.com/news/special-reports/a-guide-to-common-core/articles/2014/03/06/the-politics-of-common-core.

19.   "Texas is on the right": Ibid.

20.   "Hoosier's have high": Ibid.

21. "open the floodgates": Ibid.

22. "most important goal": Susan Berry, "Civil Disobedience: IRefuse! The Great American Opt Out from Common Core," Brietbart.com, March 29, 2014, http://www.breitbart.com/Big-Government/2014/03/26/ Civil-Disobedience-iRefuse-The-Great-American-Opt-Out-From -Common-Core.

23. "it's causing some": Ibid.

24. "be on the . . . created different": Alexander, "Common Core Curriculum: A Look Behind the Curtain of Hidden Language."

25. "an unprecedented nationwide": Michelle Malkin, "Rotten to the Core: The Feds' Invasive Student Tracking Database," michellemalkin.com, March 8, 2013, http://michellemalkin.com/2013/03/08/rotten-to -the-core-the-feds-invasive-student-tracking-database/.

26. "health-care histories": Ibid.

27. "the feds want to: Pullmann, "Joy Pullmann: Data Mining Kids Crosses Line."

28. "the Department's report": Ibid.

29. "funding and mandating": Ibid.

30. "under the DOE's": Ibid.

31. "will be available": Ibid

32. "to be stored": Valerie Strauss, "$100 Million Gates-Funded Student Data Project Ends in Failure," *The Washington Post*, April 21, 2014, http:// www.washingtonpost.com/blogs/answer-sheet/wp/2014/04/21/100 -million-gates-funded-student-data-project-ends-in-failure/.

33. "this misdirected criticism": Ibid.

34. "on-ramp": Email to author from Peter Wood, March 26, 2014.

35. "some 1.7 million": Ibid.

36. "remediation is part": Ibid.

37. "the college board": Rich Lowry, "Dumbing Down the SAT," NationalReview.com, March 11, 2014, http://www.nationalreview.com/ article/373067/dumbing-down-sat-rich-lowry.

38. "of a decade-long": Ibid.

Chapter 3

1. "there is a 75 percent": Jim Hoft, "Five Years Ago Today . . . Al Gore Predicted the North Pole Will Be Ice Free in Five Years," December 13, 2013, http://www.thegatewaypundit.com/2013/12/five-years-ago-today -al-gore-predicted-the-north-pole-will-be-ice-free-in-5-years/.

2. "a chilly Arctic": David Rose, "And Now it's Cooling! Return of the Arctic Ice Cap as it Grows 29% in a Year," DailyMail.co.uk, September 7, 2013, http://www.dailymail.co.uk/news/article-2415191/And-global -COOLING-Return-Arctic-ice-cap-grows-29-year.html.

3. In the past thirty-three: Maxim Lott, "Climate Models Wildly Overestimated Global Warming, Study Finds," FoxNews.com, September 12, 2013, http://www.foxnews.com/science/2013/09/12/ climate-models-wildly-overestimated-global-warming-study-finds/.

4. 2.5 to 10 degrees: "About Climate Change," ClimateChangeEdu.eu, http://www.climatechangeedu.eu/cc/ccabout/.

5. The journal *Nature Climate Change*: Ibid.

6. In 2012, China: "Global Carbon Budget," GlobalCarbonProject.org, http://www.globalcarbonproject.org/carbonbudget/13/hl-full.htm.

7. "congress could not": Michael Bastasch, "Podesta: Congress Can't Stop Obama on Global Warming," DailyCaller.com, May 5, 2014, http:// dailycaller.com/2014/05/05/podesta-congress-cant-stop-obama-on -global-warming/#ixzz326CmsUoW.

8. "was committed to": Ibid.

9. In another decision: Massachusetts v. Environmental Protection Agency, 549 US 497 (2007).

10. "John Coequyt, head of": John Roberts, "'Secret Dealing'? Emails Show Cozy Relationships Between EPA, Environmental Groups," FoxNews. com, January 22, 2014, http://www.foxnews.com/politics/2014/01/22/ emails-show-cozy-relationship-between-epa- environmental-groups-on -keystone-coal/.

11. "Attached is a list": Ibid.

12. 50% of our: "Table 1.1 Net Generation by Energy Source: Total (All Sectors), 2004-February 2014," eia.gov, April 22, 2014, http:// www.eia.gov/electricity/monthly/epm_table_grapher.cfm?t=epmt_1_1.

13. 620 coal fired: "Frequently Asked Questions," WorldCoal.org, http:// www.worldcoal.org/resources/frequently-asked-questions/.

14. "Emissions of the six": Ibid.

15. "something that can make": Ibid.

16. "since only the": Robert M. Duncan, "New EPA Rules Will Kill Clean Coal," *The Wall Street Journal*, October 29, 2013, http://online.wsj.com/ news/articles/SB10001424052702304171804579121393922993208.

17. "again bypass Congress": Susan Crabtree, " Obama to Take Executive Action on Fuel Efficiency," WashingtonExaminer.com, February 18,

2014, http://washingtonexaminer.com/obama-to-take-executive-action
-on-fuel-efficiency/article/2544151.

18. "initiated a systematic": Coral Davenport, "Kerry Quietly Makes Priority
of Climate Pact," *The New York Times*, January 2, 2014, http://www.
nytimes.com/2014/01/03/world/asia/kerry-shifts-state-department
-focus-to-environment.html?_r=0.

19. Article 18: Obligation: Vienna Convention on the Law of Treaties,
http://www.worldtradelaw.net/misc/viennaconvention.pdf.

20. "The EPA's draft water": Bridget Johnson, "EPA Stealthily Propels
Toward Massive Power Grab of Private Property Across the US"
PJMedia.com, November 12, 2013, http://pjmedia.com/blog/
epa-stealthily-propels-toward-massive-power-grab-of-private
-property-across-the-u-s/.

21. "the agency's own": "Smith: Draft EPA Water Rule a Massive Power
Grab," Science.house.gov, September 17, 2013, http://science.house.gov/
press-release/smith-draft-epa-water-rule-massive-power-grab.

22. "slow down, and allow": Ibid.

23. "The government might": Kelley Beaucar Vlahos, "Power Grab? Pols,
States Claim New Water Reg Could Bring Feds into Your Backyard,"
FoxNews.com, November 24, 2013, http://www.foxnews.com/
politics/2013/11/24/epa-power-grab-pols-states-claim-new-reg
-could-bring-feds-into-your-backyard/.

24. "a significant nexus": Ibid.

25. "with scientific criteria": Ibid.

26. "almost entirely about": Ibid.

27. "could have significant": Ibid.

28. "definitions would be": Ibid.

29. "gain jurisdiction over": Ibid.

30. David Winkles, Farm Bureau: Ibid.

31. "The EPA's own": Ibid.

32. "restricting mobility": Vincent Carroll, "Living Streets May be a Dead
End," Denver Post, November 14, 2009, http://www.denverpost.com/
opinion/ci_13784118.

33. "a small international": "The Birth of the Club of Rome,"
ClubOfRome.org, http://www.clubofrome.org/?p=375.

34. "a common adversary": Alexander King and Bernard Schneider, The
First Global Revolution: Hyperabad; Orient Longman, 1993, p. 324.

35. "either a real one": Ibid.

36. "In searching for a new": Ibid.

37. "single minded idealists": F.A. Hayek, The Road to Serfdom, Chicago; University of Chicago, 2007, p.166.

Chapter 4

1. "belong to taxpayers": Larry Bell, "Obama's War on Drilling: Oil Surplus, Not Scarcity, is the New Regulatory Excuse," Forbes.com, March 3, 2013, http://www.forbes.com/sites/larrybell/2013/03/03/obamas-war-on-drilling-oil-surplus-not-scarcity-is-the-new-regulatory-excuse/.

2. "the Congressional Research": Ibid.

3. "survive the bureaucratic": Ibid.

4. "since President Obama": WhiteHouse.gov, http://www.whitehouse.gov/energy/securing-american-energy.

5. "Domestic oil and natural": Ibid.

6. In the last ten: "Production of Fossil Fuel from Federal and Indian Lands Fell in 2012," eia.gov, Au-gust 12, 2013, http://www.eia.gov/todayinenergy/detail.cfm?id=12491.

7. dropped by 36%: Kerry Picket, "Picket: Flashback — Oil Drilling Permits Down 36 Percent Under Obama," Washington Times, October 16, 2012, http://www.washingtontimes.com/blog/watercooler/2012/oct/16/picket-flashback-oil-drilling-permits-down-36-perc/.

8. The average wait: Timothy Gardner and Joshua Schneyer, "In Romney Plan, Oil Drilling Unfettered by Politics," Reuters.com, August 24, 2012, http://www.reuters.com/article/2012/08/24/us-energy-us-romney-idUSBRE87N0SO20120824.

9. 6.5 million barrels: Patti Domm, "US Oil Production is Nearly Even with Imports," CNBC.com, May 8, 2013, http://www.cnbc.com/id/100721958.

10. 60% of our oil: Ben Casselman, "Number of the Week: Are US Oil Imports Up or Down?" Wall Street Journal, January 12, 2013, http://blogs.wsj.com/economics/2013/01/12/number-of-the-week-are-u-s-oil-imports-up-or-down/.

11. "survive the bureaucratic": Bell, "Obama's War on Drilling: Oil Surplus, Not Scarcity, is the New Regulatory Excuse."

12. 552,000 and two million: "Summary of Hearings on Energy," November 20, 2013, http://www.agiweb.org/gap/legis113/energy_hearings_cont.html.

13. 87% of offshore: Kyle Isakower, "Oil Supply — Yes We Can," EnergyTomorrow.org, March 13, 2012, http://www.energytomorrow .org/blog/2012/march/oil-supply-yes-we-can.

14. In the last . . . just not true: "Obama's Drilling Denials," FactCheck. org, October 19, 2012, http://www.factcheck.org/2012/10/ obamas-drilling-denials/.

15. "facts, for the most part": Ibid.

16. "Obama was wrong . . . in 2011": Ibid.

17. When Congress wouldn't: "Obama's Great Alaska Shutout," *The Wall Street Journal*, October 14, 2012, http://online.wsj.com/news/articles/ SB10000872396390443768804578040873921142716?mg= reno64-wsj&url=http%3A%2F%2Fonline.wsj.com%2Farticle% 2FSB10000872396390443768804578040873921142716.html.

18. blocking drilling for up to: Ibid.

19. "most of the other": Ibid.

20. "the largest wholesale": Ibid.

21. "will cause serious harm": Ibid.

22. Feb. 4 . . . and Colorado: "American Energy Roadblocks by the Obama Administration," NaturalResources.house.gov, http://naturalresources. house.gov/roadblocks/.

23. "the disturbance of land": "Nebraska Judge Voids Governor's Right to Set Keystone XL Route," ens-newswire.com, February 11, 2014, http://ens-newswire.com/2014/02/21/ nebraska-judge-voids-governors-right-to-set-keystone-xl-route/.

24. 2 million miles: Diana Furchtogott-Roth, "Pipelines are Safest for Transportation of Oil and Gas," Manhattan-Institute.org, June 2013, http://www.manhattan-institute.org/html/ib_23.htm#.U30op1hdXwA.

25. 9% over: "GHG Emissions," OilSandsToday.com, http:// www.oilsandstoday.ca/topics/ghgemissions/Pages/default.aspx.

26. 20,000 "shovel-ready": "How Important is Oil Sands to America's Energy Future?" EnergyAnswered.org, http://energyanswered.org/ questions/how-important-is-oil-sands-to-americas-energy-future.

Chapter 5

1. 3.5 million people . . . dropped by half: Patrick F. Fagan and Robert Rector, "The Continuing Good News About Welfare Reform," Heritage.org, February 6, 2003, http://www.heritage.org/research/ reports/2003/02/the-continuing-good-news.

2. "to more work": Pete Kasperowicz, "House Votes 246-181 to Block Obama's Welfare-Work Waiver Rule," TheHill. com, March 13, 2013, http://thehill.com/blogs/floor-action/ house/288003-house-votes-to-block-obamas-welfare-work-waiver.

3. "Information Memorandum": "TANF-ACF-IM-2013 (Guidance Concerning Waiver and Expenditure Authority Under Section 1115,) ASF.HHS.gov, July 12, 2012, http://www.acf.hhs.gov/programs/ofa/ resource/policy/im-ofa/2012/im201203/im201203.

4. "What constitutes 'work'": Molly Ball, "What Obama Really Did to Welfare Reform," *The Atlantic*, August 9, 2012, http://www.theatlantic.com/politics/ archive/2012/08/ what-obama-really-did-to- wel-fare-reform/260931/.

5. " . . . without any thought": Kasperowicz, "House Votes 246-181 to Block Obama's Welfare-Work Waiver Rule."

6. "especially through a": Ibid.

7. "Waivers granted after": Robert Rector, "How Obama Has Gutted Welfare Reform," *The Washington Post*, September 6, 2012, http:// www.washingtonpost.com/opinions/how-obama-has-gutted -welfare-reform/2012/09/06/885b0092-f835-11e1-8b93-c4f4ab1c8d13 _story.html.

8. "Effectively there are no": Kiki Bradley and Robert Rector, "Obama Guts Welfare Reform," Heritage.org, July 12, 2012, http://blog. heritage.org/2012/07/12/obama-guts-welfare-reform/.

Chapter 6

1. "The Commission shall": "47 US Code 1302 — Advanced Telecommunications Incentives," Law.Cornell.edu, http:// www.law.cornell.edu/uscode/text/47/1302.

2. "It shall take": Ibid.

3. "Google's lawyers have said": Brendan Sasso, "Google Fears FCC's New Internet Powers," NationalJournal.com, February 26, 2014, http://www.nationaljournal.com/tech/ google-fears-fcc-s-new-internet-powers-20140226.

4. "the FCC could": Ibid.

5. "very troubling": Ibid.

6. "could impose privacy": Ibid.

7. the order of Google's search: Ibid.

8. "app stores, smart-home": Ibid.

9. "No matter how . . . a problem": Edward Wyatt, "F.C.C. Seeks a New Path on 'Net Neutrality' Rules," *The New York Times*, February 19, 2014, http://www.nytimes.com/2014/02/20/business/fcc-to-propose-new -rules-on-open-internet.html?_r=0.

10. "I am deeply": Mike Snider, "FCC to Craft New Open Internet Rules," *USA Today*, February 19, 2014, http://www.usatoday.com/story/ tech/2014/02/19/fcc-proposes-open-internet-approach/5607129/.

11. "does not provide": Wyatt, "F.C.C. Seeks a New Path on 'Net Neutrality' Rules."

12. "not just to regulate": Ibid.

13. "In the wake": "Commissioner Pai Statement on FCC Internet Regulation," FCC.gov, February 19, 2014, http://www.fcc.gov/ document/commissioner-pai-statement-fcc-internet-regulation.

14. "undertake appropriate measures": Timothy B. Lee, "Authoritarian Regimes Push for Larger ITU Role in DNS System," ArsTechnica.com, December 8, 2012, http://arstechnica.com/tech-policy/2012/12/ authoritarian-regimes-push-for-larger-itu-role-in-dns-system/.

15. "some government could": Reporters Without Borders, "Internet Future at Stake at ITU-Run Dubai Conference," Trust.org, December 10, 2012, http://www.trust.org/item/20121210152700-4xm70?view=print.

16. "to access the content": "Glossary," Surveillance.RSF.org, http:// surveillance.rsf.org/en/glossary/.

17. "the confidentiality of": Reporters Without Borders, "Internet Future at Stake at ITU-Run Dubai Conference."

18. "announced plans to relinquish": Craig Timberg, "US to Relinquish Remaining Control Over the Internet," *The Washington Post*, March 14, 2014, http://www.washingtonpost.com/business/technology/us-to -relinquish-remaining-control-over-the-internet/2014/03/14/ 0c7472d0-abb5-11e3-adbc-888c8010c799_story.html.

19. "ensures that the various": Ibid.

20. "the practical consequences": Ibid.

21. "risks foreign dictatorships": Ibid.

22. "needs — and deserves": Erin Mershon and Jessica Meyers, "Internet Transition Triggers GOP Backlash," Politico.com, March 15, 2014, http://www.politico.com/story/2014/03/internet-transition-triggers -gop-backlash-104698.html.

23. "there are people": Ibid.

Index